Honorary Chairman
The Right Honorable Stephen Harper
Prime Minister of Canada

Honorary Co-Chairman
The Honorable George H.W. Bush
1996 Honorary Chairman

The Presidents Committee

Jim Armstrong	Augusta National Golf Club
The Honorable Jean Charest	Premier of Quebec
Peter Dawson	Royal & Ancient Golf Club
Tim Finchem	Commissioner, PGA TOUR
Kyi Hla Han	Asian Tour
Kym Hougham	Chairman, TAC
Johan Immelman	Commissioner, Sunshine Tour
Richard A. Janes	Commissioner, Canadian Tour
Sandy Jones	Chairman, PGA of Europe
Henrique Lavie	Commissioner, Tour de las Americas
George O'Grady	Executive Director, PGA European Tour
Michael Richards	Royal Montreal Golf Club
Ben Sellenger	CEO, Australasian Tour
Kosaku Shimada	Chairman, Japan Golf Tour Organization
The Honorable Gérald Tremblay	Mayor of Montreal
Garry West	President, Royal Canadian Golf Association
Brian Whitcomb	President, PGA of America

Tournament Staff

Mike Bodney	Senior Vice President, The Presidents Cup
Tom Clark	Executive Director
Greg Carlson	Operations Manager
Stephen Nutt	Operations Manager
Todd Tatarak	Operations Manager
Lindsey Wagner	Tournament Services Coordinator
Loredana Romanelli	Volunteer Coordinator
Kelly Abdelhay	Tournament Services Assistant
Dominic Racine	Operations Assistant

Match Committee

Steve Carman	PGA TOUR
Mike Davis	USGA
Peter Dawson	Royal & Ancient Golf Club
Jim Duncan	PGA TOUR
Mark Dusbabek	PGA TOUR
Randy Korn	Canadian Tour
Andrew Langford-Jones	PGA Tour of Australasia
Theo Manyama	Southern Africa Tour
Jack McDonald	RCGA
John Mutch Jr.	PGA TOUR
John Paramor	European Tour
David Parkin	Asian Tour
Fred Ridley	The Masters
Steve Rintoul	PGA TOUR
Mark Russell	PGA TOUR
Mike Shea	PGA TOUR
Russell Swanson	PGA Tour of Australasia
Andy Yamanaka	Japan Golf Tour Organization

Official Observer

Peter Thomson	1996/1998/2000 Presidents Cup Captain

Rules Observers

Claire Beaubien	RCGA
Martin Blake	RCGA
Jean-Claude Gagne	RCGA
Melodie Lawrek	RCGA
Thomas McCarthy	RCGA
Jacques Nols	RCGA
Dean Ryan	RCGA
Michel St-Laurent	RCGA
Grover Walker	USGA

Honorary Observer

His Excellency David Wilkins	U.S. Ambassador to Canada

The Royal Montreal Golf Club
Montreal, Quebec, Canada
25-30 September 2007

Contents

ROLEX

Forewords

It has been such an honor and a privilege to be the Captain of the International Team at The Presidents Cup. What has made it all the more special is the spirit in which every match has been played and, of course, that I have been able to be the opposing captain to my great friend and rival for so many years, Jack Nicklaus.

After The Presidents Cup in my home country of South Africa in 2003, I didn't think it could possibly get any better; but in 2005 and in 2007, the competition has been just as exciting.

On paper, it looked as though we had the team to win in 2007, but isn't golf a funny game? It just goes to show that you can throw away the form books and the statistics when 24 of the world's best golfers go head-to-head with so much commitment and great sportsmanship. That, for me, has been the highlight of all three Presidents Cups. And, to have Canadian hero Mike Weir perform so well was extremely special.

I have enjoyed every minute with my team and my Captain's Assistant, Ian Baker-Finch, both inside the ropes and inside the team rooms — they are all a great credit to this wonderful game.

Golf is blessed with many great sponsors who have ensured that the professional game continues to grow. To Rolex, thank you for recording so many great memories of The Presidents Cup in this book.

I had the pleasure of serving my fourth stint as United States Captain for The Presidents Cup. Just when I thought it could not get any better, Montreal provided not only an encore, it provided a memory that stands alone and one I will cherish forever.

The golf was spectacular; the sportsmanship even better. It was spirited yet friendly competition, and no person embodied all those positive values more than Gary Player. I have been blessed to call him a friend for over 40 years, and was fortunate to captain against him in the last three matches.

The memories I took away from Montreal didn't just take place inside the ropes. They took place outside the ropes and behind the closed doors of a team cabin. It was watching 12 special players display that they are just as special men, husbands and fathers. It was watching 12 individuals bond into one team.

The opportunity to get to know closely those 12 remarkable young men — make that 13, thanks to Captain's Assistant Jeff Sluman — was perhaps the greatest honor associated with being U.S. Captain. I love this game, and when I look at those men, and equally those of the International Team, I know that the future of golf is in good hands.

Thanks to Rolex for presenting The Presidents Cup of 2007 in this book, and for our years of shared friendship through the game of golf.

Former U.S. President George H.W. Bush and Canadian Prime Minister Stephen Harper (above) pose with The Presidents Cup between Captains Jack Nicklaus and Gary Player.

Opening Ceremony

On a warm, sun-splashed Wednesday afternoon The Presidents Cup came to Canada. Prime Minister Stephen Harper and George H.W. Bush, the former President of the United States, were on hand at The Royal Montreal Golf Club for the Opening Ceremony.

This was the seventh staging of The Presidents Cup, involving the U.S. and International Teams, which began in 1994 at Robert Trent Jones Golf Club in Virginia, and the third outside the U.S., following contests in Australia in 1998 and South Africa in 2003.

The choice of the venue was appropriate because Royal Montreal was the first golf club established in North America, chartered in 1873. Queen Victoria sanctioned the "Royal" prefix in 1884 to signify its status in the game. The modern-day club has three courses, the Blue, the Red and a nine-hole course. The Presidents Cup was played on the 7,171-yard Blue course, which opened for play in 1959 and has been host to eight Canadian Opens.

The master of ceremonies for the Opening Ceremony was Michel Lacroix, the prominent broadcaster. Leading the procession was the Black Watch–Royal Highland Regiment of Canada, followed by David Wilkins, U.S. Ambassador to Canada, and the Official Observer, three-time International Captain Peter Thomson. The Presidents Committee was led by Tim Finchem, Commissioner of the PGA TOUR, and Jean Charest, Premier of Quebec.

La Compagnie franche de la Marine de Montreal (fife and drum corps) marched in and continued playing while the two teams entered. The Royal Canadian Mounted Police Ride arrived next.

The raising of the flags — in order of the U.S., Argentina, Australia, Fiji, South Africa, South Korea and Canada — then took place, with the anthems played by La Musique Du 34ieme Groupe – Brigade Du Canada. The U.S. and Canadian anthems were also sung by Les Petits Chanteurs de Laval et Les Voix Boreales (children's choir).

Commissioner Finchem introduced U.S. Captain Jack Nicklaus, who presented his team. Johan Immelman, Commissioner of the Sunshine Tour, introduced International Captain Gary Player, who presented his team. Both captains promised none of the bitter rivalry that at times has plagued other of golf's team events. "The will to win runs deep this week, but the goodwill runs deeper," Nicklaus said.

Player paid tribute to Nicklaus for the memorable 2003 Presidents Cup in South Africa, Player's home country, which ended in a tie under a setting sun after an extra-holes showdown.

Concluding his introductions with Mike Weir, Player referred to Weir as "the pride of Canada." Player added: "You've got an International side here, but this week we are going to be 12 Canadians."

The final speakers were President Bush, who has attended every Presidents Cup except the first year, and Prime Minister Harper. The official portraits were taken before the parties exited to more music.

—Bev Norwood

FIRST DAY

U.S. Team Has Royal Start

Tiger Woods didn't wink, but he might as well have. That familiar grin was there, though — and why not? The Americans had just gotten the seventh Presidents Cup off to a rollicking start by winning five matches in the opening round of Foursomes and halving the other with a concession at Royal Montreal's 18th hole.

"We've been on this side in the last two Ryder Cups," Woods said, feigning innocence and pausing for effect before delivering the punch line. "Oh … it's the European side."

Yes, the Americans who have notoriously struggled in the alternate-shot format at the Ryder Cup played it masterfully on this cool, damp Thursday afternoon. The 30-minute rain delay that began the biennial competition was about the only thing that managed to put the brakes on the inspired Yanks.

"Needless to say, if you would say if this is what I expected the results to be, I would say no," United States Captain Jack Nicklaus would later tell the media. "But am I happy with them? Absolutely I'm happy with them. Our guys played well. They played well down the stretch.

"Time after time, they just did what they were supposed to do, and (International Captain) Gary (Player) was right, it was very close. Could have gone either way. There's a lot of golf to be played. We've got a full four-day tournament in front of us, a four-round tournament in front of us, so a lot of things can happen."

On Thursday, though, the Americans made sure that they got off to a good start in the competition, which had famously ended in a tie in 2003 and two years later ended with a U.S. win when Chris DiMarco birdied the 18th hole in the final Singles match.

Hunter Mahan, one of three players on the U.S. Team with no international team experience as a professional, wasted no time in setting the tone for the afternoon when he rolled in an 18-foot birdie putt on the first hole of the first match. As a result, he and Steve Stricker never trailed in their match with Australians Adam Scott and Geoff Ogilvy — both ranked among the top 10 in the world — that ended 3 and 2 with a U.S. birdie on the 16th hole.

Not that it was a cakewalk — far from it. Four of the afternoon's six matches reached the 18th hole, but the Americans controlled two of them on that tee and Rory Sabbatini's drive into the water paved the way for the 1-up victory by Stewart Cink and Zach Johnson in a third.

The abundance of red-white-and-blue on the leaderboards that peeked out from the colorful autumn foliage at Royal Montreal could not have been lost on the International Team. In four of the day's six matches, the Internationals only led a total of two holes, but Scott saw that dominance as reason to hunker down.

"If you're struggling out there and you see your teammates down, you don't throw in the towel," Scott

---

Steve Stricker (opposite) and Hunter Mahan put the U.S. in front.

Mike Weir carried Canada's hopes into the matches.

Gary and Vivian Player applauded a good shot.

said. "You've got to grit your teeth and get on with it. I think all our matches got off to a pretty ordinary start and we all fought back hard.

"You know, when it came down to the end we didn't come up with the big shots like the U.S. Team seemed to or the big putts."

The day's second match, though, could have gone either way until Phil Mickelson and Woody Austin, at the urging of Nicklaus, conceded a 43-inch putt at No. 18 to halve with Vijay Singh and Canada's Mike Weir. In an extremely balanced affair, each team won six holes and the Americans rallied from 3 down over the final seven with Austin's successful 13-footer on No. 18 setting the stage for the sportsmanlike display.

"When you're in the match, you don't think about it, but Captain Nicklaus said it was the right thing to do," said Mickelson, who had made a 20-footer at the 17th to keep the Americans alive. "It was a hard-fought battle. There didn't need to be a winner or loser, and Vijay is not going to miss that putt."

"It was a great match," Weir agreed. "That was probably, in the four Cups I've played in, probably the toughest match; back and forth, they got ahead and then we stormed back and then they stormed back, and it was just seesaw. So it was a number of quality shots out there, a number of quality putts holed, especially coming down our last three holes."

By the time Woods and Charles Howell III teed off in the final match of the day, the U.S. led in three matches. The U.S. twosome did their part, too, winning the 16th and 17th to dispatch K.J. Choi and Nick O'Hern, who had twice beaten the game's No. 1 in individual competition at the World Golf Championships–Accenture Match Play Championship.

The pairing of Woods and Howell was typical of Nicklaus's desire to form teams with players who wanted to play together — and in this case, the strategy paid particular dividends. The two have known each other since Howell was 16 and played Woods in the U.S. Amateur.

"My glasses were bigger than my waist size at the time and I was playing this guy named Tiger Woods who hit it 330 in the air, with the equipment then, was unbelievable, and I was in awe," recalled the rail-thin Howell, who now lives in the same Orlando development as his good friend.

Howell had broken a five-year victory drought earlier in 2007 when he out-dueled Mickelson in a playoff at the Nissan Open. After posting five top-10s in his first seven starts, though, Howell didn't have another in his next 18 leading into The Presidents Cup.

At a team meeting during the Deutsche Bank Championship, Nicklaus even jokingly told Howell he needed a lesson and Howell took the bait good-naturedly, suggesting the next morning before his 7 a.m. tee time. Woods, though, proved to be the perfect partner — Howell said his friend has a "calming effect" on him — and when the day's finale was done, the U.S. led 5½ to ½.

Asked to assess the mood in the team room as the shadows lengthened Thursday afternoon, Scott didn't mince words.

"I don't think it was so much down. (Irritated) is more the word," the young Aussie said. "If anything, it's got people pretty fired up for tomorrow. We were all just speaking about pairings for tomorrow. You know, there's stuff to sort out and a job to be done.

"If anyone was dragging their chin on the ground in there, he was told to pick it up quick and look forward to tomorrow."

As pleased as he was with the outcome, Woods was also wary.

"We're a long ways away from the end of this thing, there are so many points available," Woods said. "Second session tomorrow, you know they are going to come out with some of their best pairings and top guys out early and try to turn this thing around. We need to still go out there and play well and get our points."

—Helen Ross

Phil Mickelson and Woody Austin celebrated a birdie on No. 17.

Jack Nicklaus (center) talked with Jim Furyk and Tiger Woods.

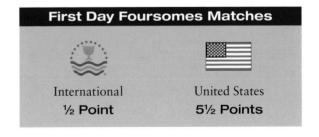

First Day Foursomes Matches

International	United States
½ Point	**5½ Points**

First Day Foursomes Match 1

Steve Stricker / Hunter Mahan
won 3 and 2 over
Adam Scott / Geoff Ogilvy

Hunter Mahan was first off in the 2007 Presidents Cup.

Adam Scott helped keep the match close.

The Americans secured the first point of The Presidents Cup in the first match by seizing the lead on the first hole and injecting a shot of confidence into a U.S. Team that could have come in with heavy doubts after its second straight disheartening Ryder Cup loss to Europe just one year earlier.

Rookie Hunter Mahan was the man who put the Americans on the right path. He drained an 18-foot birdie putt at the par-4 first hole to give himself and teammate Steve Stricker an early foothold. Stricker, playing in his first match in 11 years, took care of the tail end of the proceedings when he sank putts of eight and 12 feet to win the last two holes to close out a dynamite International Team of Australians Adam Scott and Geoff Ogilvy for a 3-and-2 decision.

The International Team struggled a bit in the alternate-shot format, hitting only five fairways and

eight greens, but the Aussies, close friends on and off the course, still held it together to make it hard on the Americans, who missed their share of fairways.

The Aussie pair was as much as 3 down after bogeys at Nos. 3 and 5, but Ogilvy, the 2006 U.S. Open champion, ignited a run of three birdies in four holes when he dropped an 11-footer. Scott rammed in a 25-foot snaking putt at No. 9 to cut the deficit to one, but then the two Aussies gave it back with a wayward drive and equally poor second shot that resulted in a bogey at the 10th.

That proved to be a crucial turning point, Stricker said.

"Getting one back at No. 10 really helped and kind of got the momentum back on our side with 2 up and eight to play," said the veteran, who last played in The Presidents Cup in 1996. "I felt comfortable the

Gary Player paired two Australians.

Geoff Ogilvy ignited a birdie run.

Jack Nicklaus praised Mahan.

way we were playing and giving ourselves opportunities for birdies. Hunter was rolling the ball great and I think we complemented each other very well."

Scott, who lost for the first time in Foursomes, managed to birdie the 11th from 13 feet, which got them back to within one, but that was as close as the International Team could get as Scott continued to fight his swing. They barely saved par with an eight-footer after a wild tee shot at the par-3 13th, and at the 15th, Stricker's bogey putt from eight feet won the hole when Scott flared his second from the middle of the fairway way off target to the right, leading to a double bogey.

At the 16th, with U.S. Captain Jack Nicklaus looking on, Mahan's approach settled inside Scott's, and Stricker wasted no time rolling it in for the knockout blow.

"We had a great match and we both played well," said Mahan, who admitted to plenty of nerves on the first tee that dissipated quickly with that opening birdie. "We had the momentum rolling and fought back and it was nice to have the lead the whole day and finish the way we did."

—*Dave Shedloski*

First Day Foursomes Match 1																		
Hole	1	2	3	4	5	6	7	8	9	10	11	12	13	14	15	16	17	18
Par	4	4	4	4	3	5	3	4	4	4	4	5	3	4	4	4	3	4
Status	1 up	1 up	2 up	2 up	3 up	3 up	3 up	2 up	1 up	2 up	1 up	1 up	1 up	1 up	2 up	3 up		
Steve Stricker Hunter Mahan	3	4	4	4	3	4	3	4	4	4	4	5	3	4	5	3		
Adam Scott Geoff Ogilvy	4	4	5	4	4	4	3	3	3	5	3	5	3	4	6	4		
Status	-	-	-	-	-	-	-	-	-	-	-	-	-	-	-	-		

Steve Stricker and Hunter Mahan (U.S.) defeated Adam Scott and Geoff Ogilvy (International), 3 and 2.

First Day Foursomes Match 2

Vijay Singh / Mike Weir

halved with

Phil Mickelson / Woody Austin

Phil Mickelson assured there would not be a loser.

A match fit to be tied ended by making a point, representing the epitome of competition and sportsmanship, not just in The Presidents Cup but also for any golf match.

Phil Mickelson and Woody Austin staged a dramatic rally over the closing holes in their Foursomes match against Vijay Singh and Canada's favorite golfing son, Mike Weir, and then extended a hand of concession to ensure that a hotly contested golf exhibition ended without a loser. The par putt that Singh sized up on the 18th hole was nearly four feet, but Mickelson and Austin, prompted by Captain Jack Nicklaus, decided that he didn't need to putt out.

"There shouldn't have been a winner or a loser," Mickelson said after the tie that provided the International Team with its only source of scoring on the first day. "It was one of the coolest and best matches I've ever been involved with."

"What a match," Weir said. "All the way around, we all had our chances. A tie was probably justified given the way it went."

The U.S. duo was 2 up early, watched the Internationals go on a remarkable tear of five wins in seven

First Day Foursomes Match 2																		
Hole	1	2	3	4	5	6	7	8	9	10	11	12	13	14	15	16	17	18
Par	4	4	4	4	3	5	3	4	4	4	4	5	3	4	4	4	3	4
Status	1 up	1 up	2 up	2 up	1 up	AS	AS	-	-	-	-	-	-	AS	-	-	AS	AS
Phil Mickelson Woody Austin	3	4	4	4	4	5	3	4	5	4	5	4	3	3	4	4	2	4
Vijay Singh Mike Weir	4	4	5	4	3	4	3	3	4	4	3	5	4	4	3	4	3	4
Status	-	-	-	-	-	AS	AS	1 up	2 up	2 up	3 up	2 up	1 up	AS	1 up	1 up	AS	AS

Phil Mickelson and Woody Austin (U.S.) halved with Vijay Singh and Mike Weir (International).

Woody Austin holed the putt on No. 18.

Mike Weir and Vijay Singh were ahead with two holes to play.

holes to fall behind by three, then mounted a wild and seemingly unlikely rally. Both sides played exceptionally, and all four men had their moments to shine; they halved only six holes, while each side won six. They combined for eight birdies.

The fireworks started on the opening hole when Austin, a rookie at age 43, sank a 30-foot birdie putt. When the International duo bogeyed the third after Weir missed the green, the crowd was silent and Mickelson and Austin were pumping fists.

The Internationals responded with their own run with Weir as the catalyst. His wedge from 110 yards at the par-5 sixth set up a kick-in birdie that leveled the match. He then drained a 16-foot birdie at No. 8 for the lead. Another laser at No. 11 from 186 yards stopped four feet away for yet another Singh birdie, and combined with a U.S. bogey at the ninth, it appeared as if the home crowd was going to be dispersed early.

Not so fast, said the Americans.

Austin sank a must-have 25-foot birdie at the par-5 12th to cut into the deficit. After the Internationals bogeyed the 13th, Mickelson took his turn by setting up Austin with an easy three-footer for birdie

at the 14th to make it three straight U.S. wins and a match restored to even.

Singh helped the home squad retake the advantage when he scooped out a bunker shot into the hole at the par-4 15th, but Austin nailed a 13-foot par save at the 16th to remain within one. Mickelson followed up by holing a 20-foot birdie on the par-3 17th to square the match one more time after Weir just missed birdie from off the front of the green. As soon as Mickelson's ball disappeared, Austin raced excitedly to the cup and plucked it out for his partner.

That set up all the dramatics at No. 18 and that's when the pressure manifested in poor swings. Both Austin and Singh missed the green. Mickelson splashed out of the bunker to 13 feet. Weir chipped to four feet. Austin proved he was up to the task one more time, burying the putt. Nicklaus then sidled up to his charges and broached the subject of conceding the par to the International Team.

"They jumped right on it," Nicklaus said. "They deserve the credit. Given the circumstances, it was the right thing to do."

—Dave Shedloski

First Day Foursomes Match 3

Stewart Cink / Zach Johnson
won 1 up over

Rory Sabbatini / Trevor Immelman

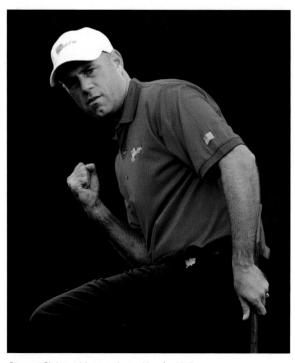

Stewart Cink put his team in position for birdies.

Zach Johnson and Cink had three sand saves.

Stewart Cink and Zach Johnson were on each other's lists. The lists U.S. Captain Jack Nicklaus asked his players to write: Who do you want to play with? Who do you not want to play with?

And, honestly, there was no keeping those two Americans apart. They played together in the 2005 World Cup and finished 17th. They were paired again in the 2006 Ryder Cup with disastrous results, losing to Paul Casey and David Howell 5 and 4.

Their debut at Royal Montreal had a happier ending — a 1-up victory over the South African combination of Rory Sabbatini and Trevor Immelman for the Americans' second full point on the first day of The Presidents Cup.

"That's the first good thing we've done, I think, in history," Cink said. "We're real pleased to get one on the good side."

It was anything but easy, with Cink pushing the opening drive into the woods and with Johnson putting the team in difficult positions all day. Cink held this one together with some great shots that gave Johnson the chances to hole the putts. There was an eight-foot birdie at the seventh, a 16-footer at the eighth and a 22-footer at the 12th from Johnson, and three sand saves.

"I leaned on him a lot," Johnson said, "and fortunately we were able to come through."

As with any match, timing is just about everything, and the Americans had it. The Internationals didn't.

Sabbatini and Immelman won the first two holes to take a 2-up lead with Sabbatini's 19-footer, but couldn't hang on as Johnson came back to sink huge putts at the seventh and eighth holes to square the match. After the U.S. took the lead back at the 12th, Sabbatini squared it at the 14th. Johnson kept the U.S. in the match at the 16th to set the stage for a soggy finish to a soggier day.

Standing on the 18th tee with a chance to come away with a halve or a win, Sabbatini wound up with his driver and let one fly — straight into the water that hugs the left side of the fairway. That meant the match was, basically, over.

"He's long off the tee and he can reach the bunker on the right, and now, you've got the water," International Captain Gary Player said. "That's a driver. You mustn't go with a driver. You've got to go with a 3-wood because you can aim it at the trap and not hit it. It makes the fairway a lot wider if you go that way."

Sabbatini, who made the first of three crucial International errors at No. 18 on the first day, agreed. He said: "It was in my mind and I just made the wrong decision."

The two teams wound up conceding each other's final putts — the U.S. conceded a longer bogey for the Internationals first — but all the Americans needed was a safe par and they got it.

Cink was surprised that the Internationals conceded his putt. "You always expect to have to putt," he said. "Especially to win the match. But I didn't think it was right to make them, you know, have to putt out theirs. And that was a good show of sportsmanship from both sides."

—*Melanie Hauser*

Trevor Immelman and Rory Sabbatini won the first two holes.

First Day Foursomes Match 3

Hole	1	2	3	4	5	6	7	8	9	10	11	12	13	14	15	16	17	18
Par	4	4	4	4	3	5	3	4	4	4	4	5	3	4	4	4	3	4
Status	-	-	-	-	-	-	-	AS	AS	AS	AS	1 up	1 up	AS	AS	AS	AS	1 up
Stewart Cink Zach Johnson	5	4	4	4	3	4	2	3	4	4	4	4	3	4	4	4	3	4
Rory Sabbatini Trevor Immelman	4	3	4	4	3	4	3	4	4	4	4	5	3	3	4	4	3	5
Status	1 up	2 up	2 up	2 up	2 up	2 up	1 up	AS	AS	AS	AS	-	-	AS	AS	AS	AS	-

Stewart Cink and Zach Johnson (U.S.) defeated Rory Sabbatini and Trevor Immelman (International), 1 up.

First Day Foursomes Match 4

David Toms / Jim Furyk

won 1 up over

Ernie Els / Angel Cabrera

It started off so easy for David Toms and Jim Furyk.

Birdies on two of the first three holes, a 2-up lead after four holes. It seemed as though America's quiet men just might take down the long-hitting Internationals quickly. Quickly enough to grab the first point.

But no.

Ernie Els did indeed lose his opening match for the third time in four Presidents Cups, but he and

Jim Furyk and David Toms were happy to secure a point.

Angel Cabrera went down swinging at the 18th hole when Els missed a four-footer that would have halved the match.

Call it the second International unforced error of the day at No. 18. Furyk, after all, had handed the Internationals a chance to steal the match when he put his tee shot in the lake down the left of the 18th fairway. But Toms scrambled to put the team in position to two-putt for bogey, dropping the winning four-footer himself.

It was quite the turnaround from earlier when the Americans lost only one of the first 10 holes and were 3 up going to the 11th tee. They were 1 up after the fifth hole, then stretched the lead to 3 up courtesy of Toms's approach at the eighth hole which landed 11 inches from the pin, and an International bogey at the 10th. Just when it seemed the U.S. might be putting another match out of reach, Cabrera and Els birdied the 12th and 14th holes and the U.S. bogeyed the 15th to cut the lead to one.

"Definitely it was a very good comeback," Cabrera said. "We were 2 down and we were actually playing quite well. It was a good comeback, but miss-

First Day Foursomes Match 4																		
Hole	1	2	3	4	5	6	7	8	9	10	11	12	13	14	15	16	17	18
Par	4	4	4	4	3	5	3	4	4	4	4	5	3	4	4	4	3	4
Status	AS	AS	1 up	2 up	1 up	1 up	1 up	2 up	2 up	3 up	3 up	2 up	3 up	2 up	1 up	1 up	1 up	1 up
David Toms Jim Furyk	4	3	3	4	3	4	3	3	4	4	4	5	2	4	5	4	3	5
Ernie Els Angel Cabrera	4	3	4	5	2	4	3	4	4	5	4	4	3	3	4	4	3	5
Status	AS	AS	-	-	-	-	-	-	-	-	-	-	-	-	-	-	-	-

David Toms and Jim Furyk (U.S.) defeated Ernie Els and Angel Cabrera (International), 1 up.

Angel Cabrera admitted being frustrated.

ing the last putt and being without a point keeps me, you know, a little bit frustrated."

The Internationals started their comeback with a win at the 12th hole, but after Toms made an 18-footer at the 13th hole, the U.S. was 3 up again. This time with five holes to play. Then Els came out of the bunker to give Cabrera a short putt to cut the lead to two. Furyk found the water off the tee at No. 15 and the Internationals two-putted to cut the lead to 1 up and set the stage for the 18th-hole roller coaster ride.

Then, Furyk found the water off the tee again at the 18th. Toms put them in position to two-putt for bogey, while the Internationals three-putted for their bogey when Els ran a four-footer past the hole. The U.S. conceded the putt.

"We gave away a couple there at the end, but it was good enough for a win," Toms said.

A quip from Player, who was still shaking his head over his long hitters being stymied by Toms and Furyk: "That's a little bit of David and Goliath there, isn't it? They hit it about 50 yards by both of them, don't they?"

But that didn't matter. Missed putts did.

"I felt terrible for Ernie, missing the short putt he missed," Nicklaus said. "He's holed so many putts because he needed to. ... It looked to me like he thought the ball was going to break right and he missed it on the left side of the hole."

—*Melanie Hauser*

Ernie Els had a four-footer for a halve, but missed.

First Day Foursomes Match 5

Lucas Glover / Scott Verplank

won 2 up over

Stuart Appleby / Retief Goosen

Stuart Appleby relied on match experience.

Rookie Lucas Glover provided length off the tees.

Foursomes are quirky. And, quite often, not the least bit comfortable. Unless, of course, you've got a friend by your side.

Just ask Lucas Glover. The American rookie opened his Presidents Cup career beside Scott Verplank. It was a pairing of two distinctly different games — Glover hits it a mile; Verplank just finds fairways and makes putts — and two very good friends.

"We know each other pretty well and we've played a lot of golf together and we've talked about playing together in this deal," Verplank said. "We're very comfortable. I think that a big part of it is getting comfortable with your partner and having fun."

They play practice rounds together. Go out to dinner together on the road. And together, they picked up America's fourth full point of the first day with a 2-up win over Stuart Appleby and Retief Goosen.

Sound easy? Well, Captain Jack Nicklaus did find the perfect partner to keep Glover calm and focused by pairing him with a player who finished the day with an unbeaten Foursomes record (2-0-1) in The Presidents Cup. But there wasn't much easy in this one.

The Americans faced two very experienced players in Goosen, who came in with a 9-5-1 record, and Appleby, who was 3-11-2 to open the matches, and it was another dogfight.

Glover's wake-up call came on the first hole when he missed an eight-foot putt to give the hole to the Internationals. He bounced right back to square the match, holing a 15-footer for birdie at the second, and the Americans never trailed again.

After three-putting the fifth hole from 49 feet, Goosen provided a thrill at No. 6 when he holed a 40-

foot bunker shot for eagle to square the match once again. Verplank stiffed his tee shot at the seventh, but the Internationals tied it up again at the eighth.

The turning point came at No. 15 when Glover's approach stopped six feet from the hole and Verplank rolled it in. The rookie added a 12-footer at the 16th to put the U.S. up by two with two holes to play, but the experienced Internationals weren't backing down.

Goosen sent the match to No. 18 when he sank a nine-footer from the fringe for a birdie at No. 17, but it wasn't enough. Appleby pulled his approach for the third International error there in three matches. Glover picked it out of the bunker and Verplank was conceded the putt for the win.

"If we got two out of those three on the 18th," Adam Scott said of watching his team's errors unfold, "it would have been a bit closer, but obviously the 18th hole means a lot when matches come to it."

So does having a good friend beside you.

"I feel whoever my partner is, we're going to be competitive," Verplank said. "I think he knows I'm probably going to hit the fairway. They may be a bit farther back than they're used to, but they're going to have a good lie. They generally know I'm going to make most of the critical putts. I'm generally pretty good with a putter from six or eight feet and in, which you have a lot of to halve holes, sometimes to win."

—*Melanie Hauser*

Retief Goosen's putting kept his team in the match.

Scott Verplank (left) laughed with Jack Nicklaus and Glover.

First Day Foursomes Match 5

Hole	1	2	3	4	5	6	7	8	9	10	11	12	13	14	15	16	17	18
Par	4	4	4	4	3	5	3	4	4	4	4	5	3	4	4	4	3	4
Status	-	AS	AS	AS	1 up	AS	1 up	AS	AS	AS	AS	AS	AS	AS	1 up	2 up	1 up	2 up
Lucas Glover Scott Verplank	5	3	4	4	3	-	2	4	4	5	4	5	3	4	3	3	3	C
Stuart Appleby Retief Goosen	4	4	4	4	4	3C	3	3	4	5	4	5	3	4	4	4	2	-
Status	1 up	AS	AS	AS	-	AS	-	AS	AS	AS	AS	AS	AS	AS	-	-	-	-

Lucas Glover and Scott Verplank (U.S.) defeated Stuart Appleby and Retief Goosen (International), 2 up.

First Day Foursomes Match 6

Tiger Woods / Charles Howell III
won 3 and 1 over

K.J. Choi / Nick O'Hern

Tiger Woods kept hitting the greens.

Reprising a successful Foursomes team from 2003, Jack Nicklaus paired Tiger Woods with a player who can hit it as far as the No. 1 player in the world and who lives near the top American as a neighbor in Orlando, Florida.

Charles Howell III, back in the American fold, assisted Woods in his first alternate-shot triumph since their 2003 pairing as they posted a rather scraggly but still pleasing 3-and-1 victory over K.J. Choi and Nick O'Hern.

Neither team putted well, but the Americans hit a few more greens, and that was the difference.

Things certainly didn't start well for the visitors. Woods popped up his first tee shot high into the air, carrying it just 233 yards and well short of the short-hitting O'Hern, who has been something of a nemesis for Woods, having defeated him twice in three years in the World Golf Championships–Accenture Match Play Championship. That hole was halved, but an American miscue at the fourth led to a bogey and loss of the hole.

Woods sank a 14-foot par putt at the fifth to

First Day Foursomes Match 6

Hole	1	2	3	4	5	6	7	8	9	10	11	12	13	14	15	16	17	18
Par	4	4	4	4	3	5	3	4	4	4	4	5	3	4	4	4	3	4
Status	AS	AS	AS	-	AS	1 up	1 up	1 up	1 up	2 up	1 up	1 up	1 up	2 up	1 up	2 up	3 up	
Tiger Woods Charles Howell III	4	4	4	5	3	4	3	3	4	4	5	5	3	3	4	4	2	
K.J. Choi Nick O'Hern	4	4	4	4	4	5	3	3	4	5	4	5	3	4	3	5	3	
Status	AS	AS	AS	1 up	AS	-	-	-	-	-	-	-	-	-	-	-	-	

Tiger Woods and Charles Howell III (U.S.) defeated K.J. Choi and Nick O'Hern (International), 3 and 1.

Charles Howell III matched Woods in length.

K.J. Choi drove into the water on No. 16.

return the favor, and the Americans followed up at the par-5 sixth with their first birdie after Howell stuck a wedge to within three feet.

An exchange of bogeys at the 10th and 11th left the combatants still one apart, with Howell missing a tester of about three feet at the 11th. But Howell made up for it with an 11-footer for birdie at No. 14 to go 2 up. Howell, who converted the only two putts outside 10 feet for the Americans, said Woods was a calming presence during a tough match — just as Nicklaus suspected he might be.

"I thought that Tiger would play the steadying influence on Charles, although he's not a rookie," Nicklaus said. "And I kept kidding Charles all day. I said: 'Are you holding him in, are you keeping Tiger straight? Good going, keep holding him in.'"

O'Hern helped hold the Internationals in the match. His 14-foot birdie at the 15th — just the sec-

ond of the round for him and Choi — again cut the deficit in half. Then things got dicey. Choi squandered the International momentum when he drove in the water at No. 16, but Howell committed the same sin. He corrected the error with a four-foot par putt after a wonderful Woods approach to again go 2 up.

When Woods hit it stiff and Howell knocked in another birdie at No. 17, the U.S. had secured their fifth win of the day and Woods had improved to 6-2-1 in Foursomes.

"We got the job done today," Woods said in a matter-of-fact tone after a hard-fought decision. "Our responsibility is to go out there and get a point. We did that today and it was a lot of fun. We put the pressure on them a little bit toward the middle part of the round and didn't make any mistakes there."

—*Dave Shedloski*

Internationals Dunk Americans

Dinner on Thursday night, Vijay Singh acknowledged, didn't exactly go down too well. The Internationals had just been shellacked during the opening round of Foursomes at The Presidents Cup — winning just one measly half point. Proud men all, they were determined to change their fortunes when the biennial competition resumed with the Four-ball matches on Friday.

"We had a good talk in the bus coming over," Singh said. "I don't know if all of us were listening, but it was the talk anyway. We just wanted to get some points up there. I mean, five points down on the first day, our morale wasn't very good at the dinner last night. I think we all kind of drank a little too much and tried to drown our sorrows — or some of us did, anyway."

The Internationals refused to mope when it came time to get back to business on Friday, though. A dramatic shift in momentum resulted, too, with Captain Gary Player's team winning four matches and halving another to pull within a more manageable deficit of 7 to 5 entering Saturday's all-important double round of match play.

"We had a good talk," Weir said. "You know, we have 12 great players on our team, and we knew yesterday was a little bit of an aberration. It was closer actually than what the score indicated. We felt we had four matches go to 18 and just didn't turn our way,

Woody Austin (opposite) took a tumble into the water at No. 14 but emerged as an action hero — Aqua Man.

and we knew if we stuck to our guns today and got off to a good start, (we'd be okay)."

"This is a match now, and very exciting," Player agreed.

Singh and his partner, Stuart Appleby, got the Internationals off on the right foot with a dominating 5-and-4 win over Tiger Woods and Jim Furyk, who are ranked Nos. 1 and 3 in the world, respectively. The defeat was Woods's worst ever as a professional in match play — a drubbing Singh would later call simply "a good beating."

"I think anybody who is put up against Tiger, you say, that's going to be a tough match, no matter who is on the team," Singh said. "It was almost like, well, we probably have to lose that point at the beginning of the day, because he's playing so well and with Jim, it's going to be a hard match. So that was a point we needed."

Singh and Appleby, who had entered the match with a 3-12-2 Presidents Cup record, were on fire Friday. They went off second and played the first 14 holes in 11-under par with Singh twice holing shots and Appleby making three birdies and an eagle. Suddenly, Woods and Furyk found themselves 3 down after seven holes and they never recovered.

Mission accomplished.

"We came out strong," Singh said. "We wanted to put some points up there early and give the guys coming behind something to look up to, and give them some sort of a boost. Our match went really good. We got lucky in the first few holes. I chipped

Gary Player (left) followed play with TOUR official Sid Wilson.

Vijay Singh and Stuart Appleby got the Internationals started.

in and made a good pitch in on No. 6. Stuart played great, as well. He drove the ball beautifully, took a lot of pressure off me and we just molded perfectly.

"When I was out of the hole, he was in. We played some good golf. You know, if you look at it, 5 and 4, it looks very comfortable, but we had to work on every shot out there. It wasn't easy at all. We're just lucky to come up ahead I guess this time."

The performance of the two veterans was not lost on the rest of the International Team.

"I think obviously you look on paper, you have … Tiger playing so well, and Jim, as he said, he's never out of the hole; he's No. 3 in the world. So you have No. 1 and No. 3 in the world, they are a tough combination," said Weir, who played his first match ever with Ernie Els and defeated Zach Johnson and Charles Howell III 3 and 1.

"But Vijay has been No. 1 for a reason and Stuart has played some solid golf. You know in this format that anybody can beat anybody. But it does give the team a good boost to win a good match like that. You know, I think probably the rest of the team is looking

up on the board, and on our side we were excited to see that."

As solid as the Internationals played on Friday, though, they still were upstaged by America's loveable lug of a rookie in the 43-year-old Woody Austin.

The emotional Austin already had shown how strong his desire was down the stretch on Thursday as he made clutch par putts on the 16th and 18th holes — the first to halve the hole and the second to assure the Americans of at least a half point. During his Four-ball match with David Toms on Friday, though, the U.S. Team learned just how far Austin was willing to go to win.

Austin hit his tee shot on the 14th hole, a short, reachable par-4, into the mud on the bank beside the green. The ball was submerged, yet visible, and with his opponents, Trevor Immelman and Rory Sabbatini, within easy reach of birdie, and Toms in the water with no shot, Austin decided to try to hit the ball.

In what will forever be the SportsCenter moment of the 2007 Presidents Cup, Austin took a swipe at the ball, then did an awkward pirouette, lost his balance and tumbled head-first into the water. Phil Mickelson, who played with Austin in the first round and would be paired with him again on Saturday, dubbed him "Aqua Man" and Jack Nicklaus later announced him as Jacques Cousteau.

"It was real funny," Immelman said. "Obviously

it wasn't for him, but he took it in great spirits. It just shows what a great player he is, because he bounced back from there and got his thoughts and his emotions together and played really well."

Indeed. Austin went on to make birdie on the last three holes to assure the Americans of a half point. "I think it was a great day for Woody individually," Toms said in understatement. Not to mention, Scott Verplank, who witnessed the dive while standing on the 16th tee, said, "I think Woody, his effects were far reaching. … I watched the last few holes, it was pretty spectacular."

Austin's response was simple. "I have the mentality where I will do anything I can for my part, my teammates, whatever. I hope today I proved that I'm never going to give up until it's over," said the man who was fast becoming the heart and soul of the U.S. Team.

His captain, arguably the greatest player the game has ever seen, was impressed by what he called Austin's "pure grit down the stretch."

"The one that amazed me was Woody Austin," Nicklaus said with a smile. "Here he is, he takes a dive in a lake and then holes three straight putts. He's amazing. He's been terrific so far. We were fortunate we had yesterday's lead, because we don't have much of a lead now. Tomorrow is a big day, two rounds. It will be a difficult day, a tough day for both teams."

—*Helen Ross*

Second Day Four-ball Matches

International	United States
4½ Points	**1½ Points**

Second Day Total

International	United States
5 Points	**7 Points**

Second Day Four-ball Match 7

Angel Cabrera / Retief Goosen
won 1 up over
Phil Mickelson / Hunter Mahan

Phil Mickelson led an American comeback.

Angel Cabrera was taking no chances.

Leaves were tumbling across the 18th green, the wind whipping and the temperature was dropping by the minute. But the weather wasn't the only thing changing at Royal Montreal.

So was the momentum.

Cabrera hadn't seen a birdie putt fall since the seventh hole and, well, he and Ernie Els had lost a match at the 18th Thursday, so he was going to finish this hole on his time. He waited for the winds to calm down and then he slammed in an 11-foot putt to win the match and give the Internationals their second point of the day — a 1-up win over Phil Mickelson and Hunter Mahan in Friday's lead-off match.

Like Mickelson's Foursomes match with Woody Austin, the Americans staged a comeback in the match, only this time they fell one hole short. Mickelson squared the match at the 14th hole, but Mahan missed a 40-foot birdie putt at No. 18, opening the way for Cabrera to give the Internationals a two-for-two start in the Four-ball matches.

Second Day Four-ball Match 7																		
Hole	1	2	3	4	5	6	7	8	9	10	11	12	13	14	15	16	17	18
Par	4	4	4	4	3	5	3	4	4	4	4	5	3	4	4	4	3	4
Status	AS	AS	-	-	-	-	-	-	-	-	-	-	-	AS	AS	AS	AS	-
Phil Mickelson	4	4	4	4	4	5	2	4	4	4	4	3	3	3	4	4	3	4
Hunter Mahan	4	4	4	4	4	4	3	4	5	4	6	4	3	-	4	4	2	4
Angel Cabrera	4	4	3	4	-	4	2	4	4	4	5	4	3	-	4	4	3	3
Retief Goosen	4	4	4	5	3	-	3	4	4	4	5	3	3	4	4	4	2	-
Status	AS	AS	1 up	1 up	2 up	2 up	2 up	2 up	2 up	2 up	1 up	1 up	1 up	AS	AS	AS	AS	1 up

Angel Cabrera and Retief Goosen (International) defeated Phil Mickelson and Hunter Mahan (U.S.), 1 up.

Hunter Mahan hit to 40 feet at No. 18, but missed the putt.

Angel Cabrera rolled home an 11-foot putt to win.

"Well, we fought hard today, and unfortunately we came up a little shy," said Mickelson, who missed the green at the 18th and had a six-footer for par. "We fought hard to stay in the match and made some eagles and birdies to keep us in the match."

They made them just to get into it. Cabrera and Goosen — call this the U.S. Open champions pairing — took a 2-up lead after five holes. It could have been more had they not missed a pair of short birdies early, and they kept it until Mickelson cut the lead to one after a nine-footer for par at the 11th. It wasn't the prettiest of holes. Goosen and Cabrera both bogeyed that hole and Mahan took a double bogey.

The momentum swung at the 12th when Mickelson rolled in a long eagle putt to match Goosen's short eagle, then Mickelson squared it at No. 14. They matched each other at Nos. 15, 16 and 17, to set the stage for Cabrera's putt.

"We had a lot of fun," Mickelson said. "We enjoy playing with each other. We had a good chemistry going. He was able to hit some good shots when I wasn't. We worked well together as a team.

"Retief made a couple of shots there on us, and 18, we didn't follow their birdie and Retief was right there if (Cabrera) didn't make his putt. We came up

one hole short, but it was a fun, difficult, challenging match."

You would have expected no less. Goosen was 5-1 in this format coming into the day. Yes, Cabrera, with his lumbering gait and booming drives, was 0-0-2 in Four-ball, but was playing well.

After waiting for the wind to die down, Cabrera moved a few leaves, then stroked his putt into the middle of the hole.

—*Melanie Hauser*

Second Day Four-ball Match 8

Vijay Singh / Stuart Appleby
won 5 and 4 over
Tiger Woods / Jim Furyk

Stuart Appleby produced an eagle and four birdies.

Tiger Woods called it a spanking.

Vijay Singh called it the International Team's first full point.

And the record books? They called Singh and Stuart Appleby's 5-and-4 spotlight victory over Woods and Jim Furyk the most lopsided in the first eight matches of this Presidents Cup, and Woods's worst match-play loss — in any format — in his professional career.

This one, which came over what most would say was America's top team — not to mention the Nos. 1 and 3 players in the Official World Golf Ranking — was the start of a three-for-three start for the Internationals Friday and pushed Singh's record against Woods in Four-ball matches to 5-1.

"To beat the dream team, we didn't do it easily, but we did it decisively," said Appleby. "Obviously, Vijay came up big. We got cleaned yesterday and we needed to bounce back. Vijay set the tone."

As for the 5-and-4 score, it didn't even feel that close.

Singh mentioned something about being lucky,

Second Day Four-ball Match 8																		
Hole	1	2	3	4	5	6	7	8	9	10	11	12	13	14	15	16	17	18
Par	4	4	4	4	3	5	3	4	4	4	4	5	3	4	4	4	3	4
Status	-	-	-	-	-	-	-	-	-	-	-	-	-	-				
Tiger Woods	4	-	4	4	3	4	3	-	4	4	4	4	3	3				
Jim Furyk	4	3	3	4	3	4	3	3	4	4	4	4	3	4				
Vijay Singh	3	3	4	4	3	3	3	4	4	3	4	4	2	3				
Stuart Appleby	-	3	3	4	3	-	2	4	4	4	4	3	3	4				
Status	1 up	1 up	1 up	1 up	1 up	2 up	3 up	2 up	2 up	3 up	3 up	4 up	5 up	5 up				

Vijay Singh and Stuart Appleby (International) defeated Tiger Woods and Jim Furyk (U.S.), 5 and 4.

For Tiger Woods, a birdie on No. 14 wasn't enough.

but he holed out from off the green — one for eagle — on two of the first six holes. Appleby had an eagle and four birdies on his own ball, giving the twosome a best-ball score of 11-under par for 14 holes.

"Amazing," Captain Gary Player said, shaking his head. "Eleven-under par … what a way to win. It's just what we needed, really."

The win snapped the Internationals out of the doldrums of Thursday's matches when the Americans took a 5½-to-½ lead. Woods's previous worst loss in either Ryder or Presidents Cup history was 5 and 3 (Bernhard Langer/Colin Montgomerie beat Woods/Mark O'Meara in 1997 Ryder Cup Foursomes; Els/Tim Clark beat Woods/Howell 5 and 3 in 2003 Presidents Cup Foursomes). His worst defeat ever was a 6-and-4 loss to Tim Herron in the second round of the 1992 U.S. Amateur.

Woods made three birdies, and he and Furyk shot five-under par. Hardly enough against the red-hot Fijian, who struggled a few weeks earlier during the FedExCup run, and his Australian sidekick.

It started on the first hole when Singh short-sided himself and holed out from the bunker. It felt like déjà vu when the 33-footer rolled in, since Singh's last bunker shot went in, too — on the 14th hole of his Foursomes match with Mike Weir.

Appleby birdied the next two holes to match Furyk's birdies. Then it was Singh holing out from in front of the sixth green for eagle and Appleby birding the seventh to go 3 up.

"The way it was going, I didn't want to putt," Singh laughed. "I didn't even know how to putt until the seventh hole. But I was confident in what I was doing and relaxed playing with Stuart. We really gelled well."

A Furyk birdie on the next hole cut it to 2 up, then Singh birdied No. 10, Appleby threw in a 32-foot eagle at the 12th, and Singh birdied No. 13 to go 5 up.

Tiger made an all-world up-and-down birdie on the 14th, but it wasn't enough. Singh closed out the match with a three-foot birdie.

"They chipped in twice, 11-under par through 14 holes … that's pretty good playing," said Woods, who dropped to 2-7 in Four-ball. "We needed to take it a lot deeper, and we didn't do it."

Added Singh: "It was a good statement in one respect, because Tiger, obviously he's playing unbelievable golf, and Jim is never out of the hole. So for us to beat them, it was a good beating. At the end of the day, it was a point that really mattered."

—Melanie Hauser

Woods and Jim Furyk congratulated Vijay Singh.

Second Day Four-ball Match 9

Ernie Els / Mike Weir

won 3 and 1 over

Zach Johnson / Charles Howell III

With seven birdies, Mike Weir led the way.

On a day when the International Team needed to shine to get back into contention in The Presidents Cup, Mike Weir was one of several beacons of inspiration.

With six birdies in his first 14 holes and seven overall, Canada's beloved son brought his revamped game to life, pleasing the large and boisterous partisan crowd and picking up partner Ernie Els at crucial times as the International Team never trailed in a 3-and-1 decision over Charles Howell III and Masters champion Zach Johnson.

The victory was the third in a row and fourth overall for the International Team during Friday's second session of six Four-ball matches.

"(Weir) played some amazing golf today," said Els, who only contributed an outright birdie on one hole. "I just tried to steady the ship a bit, but Mike made the putts."

After halves between the two squads at the first six holes — three with birdies — Weir put the International Team on top for good with a wedge to the par-3 seventh that stopped two feet away. He upped

Second Day Four-ball Match 9																		
Hole	1	2	3	4	5	6	7	8	9	10	11	12	13	14	15	16	17	18
Par	4	4	4	4	3	5	3	4	4	4	4	5	3	4	4	4	3	4
Status	AS	AS	AS	AS	AS	AS	-	-	-	-	-	-	-	-	-	-	-	
Zach Johnson	4	3	4	4	2	4	3	4	4	4	5	-	3	3	4	4	3	
Charles Howell III	4	-	4	5	-	4	3	4	4	4	5	4	4	4	-	3	3	
Ernie Els	4	4	4	5	2	4	-	4	4	4	5	4	3	3	4	4	-	
Mike Weir	4	3	4	4	3	4	2	3	4	4	4	4	3	3	4	4	2	
Status	AS	AS	AS	AS	AS	AS	1 up	2 up	2 up	2 up	3 up	3 up	3 up	3 up	3 up	2 up	3 up	

Ernie Els and Mike Weir (International) defeated Zach Johnson and Charles Howell III (U.S.), 3 and 1.

Ernie Els was steady, but scored only one birdie.

the ante on the next with another wedge that checked up to six feet and his conversion doubled the advantage.

Weir, responding to the pressure of having to prove himself after being a captain's selection, said that staying with a strategy in which he hit first off the tee helped him create opportunities. His performance could not have been more inspirational. The diminutive lefty hit 12 of 13 fairways and 14 of 17 greens. He didn't suffer a bogey.

"Well, I think that was it: for me to tee off and get the ball in the fairway and then Ernie on the par-5s could take more chances," Weir said. "The strategy worked well, I was able to drive it and make birdies, and you know, just me getting into play before he can let loose."

Things got even looser for the home team when Howell and Johnson failed to make par at the 11th to slip three behind, and the U.S. duo couldn't muster any offense until they were dormie at No. 16 when Howell delivered a seven-foot birdie. That was their lone victory, and the good feeling was short-lived.

The match ended with conceded birdies at the par-3 17th for the Internationals (Weir was 20 feet away) when Howell missed the green and Johnson's long birdie attempt ran 10 feet by.

At the finish, Weir was more cognitive of what

Zach Johnson and Charles Howell III couldn't keep the pace.

the fans had contributed and not what he had done.

"It's a lot different than a typical Canadian Open week for me," Weir said. "With 11 other teammates, we're doing everything together. Obviously I've got a lot of attention on me this week, but we like to say there's 11 other adopted Canadians this week. But at the same time, to have the support that I've had this week, and walking on every hole, it just kind of gives me goose bumps actually to think about it."

—*Dave Shedloski*

Second Day Four-ball Match 10

Steve Stricker / Scott Verplank
won 2 and 1 over

Adam Scott / K.J. Choi

Steve Stricker and Scott Verplank produced the only U.S. win.

Put together two of the most consistent ball-strikers and putters in a Four-ball format and three things are likely to happen: plenty of birdies, few mistakes and an eventual victory.

The pairing of Scott Verplank and Steve Stricker produced such results for an American team that was reeling on the second day. Their efforts in a 2-and-1 win over Adam Scott and K.J. Choi accounted for the only full point for the U.S. Team.

The American veterans combined for eight birdies, with Stricker notching five of them, and they needed every last one of them to hold off the Internationals, not only in their match, but also in the overall standings that by the end of the day got close.

"As the day started to unfold, you could look at the board and see that the direction of the day was going in favor of the International Team," Stricker said. "I was looking at it, and I'm sure Scott was, too, in our match, and we felt it was very important to try to sneak out a half a point at least, if not a full. But we played well together. We supported each other. When I was out of the hole, he would pick me up and vice

Second Day Four-ball Match 10

Hole	1	2	3	4	5	6	7	8	9	10	11	12	13	14	15	16	17	18
Par	4	4	4	4	3	5	3	4	4	4	4	5	3	4	4	4	3	4
Status	1 up	1 up	1 up	1 up	1 up	2 up	1 up	AS	AS	1 up	AS	AS	AS	1 up	1 up	2 up	2 up	
Steve Stricker	4	4	4	5	3	4	3	4	4	3	4	4	3	3	4	3	3	
Scott Verplank	5	4	3	5	3	5	3	4	4	4	4	4	3	3	4	4	4	
Adam Scott	5	4	4	5	3	5	2	3	4	4	3	4	3	4	4	4	3	
K.J. Choi	5	4	3	5	3	5	-	4	5	4	4	4	3	4	4	4	-	
Status	-	-	-	-	-	-	-	AS	AS	-	AS	AS	AS	-	-	-	-	

Steve Stricker and Scott Verplank (U.S.) defeated Adam Scott and K.J. Choi (International), 2 and 1.

Adam Scott missed this birdie putt on No. 14.

pretty hard, and we both scratch and claw. And when you get guys together that almost actually enjoy doing that, then it makes for a good team."

Both Americans birdied the 14th, though it was Verplank's 20-footer that counted. More heat was applied at the tough par-4 16th when Stricker nailed a 14-footer for a birdie to leave the home pair dormie.

Needing to get the ball close at the par-3 17th, the Internationals instead got themselves in a pickle. Choi hit in the water, and Scott's approach ended up about 50 feet away. He putted splendidly to get down in two, but Stricker's perfunctory par sealed the match.

"I didn't realize (we were the only team up). I was just paying attention to our match and trying to get the job done, and fortunately we did," Stricker said.

—Dave Shedloski

versa. So we made a good team today, and we were fortunate enough to get a point."

The Americans never trailed even though they constituted by far the oldest twosome with both men over 40. Yet they never could get comfortable either. They led 2 up through six holes but found themselves tied with five to go despite their solid scorecards.

A bogey on the first and Stricker's six-foot birdie on the par-5 sixth put the International duo in that early hole, but Scott nearly aced No. 7 and he followed with a 15-foot birdie at the next to draw his team even. Stricker, from five feet, and Scott, from 22 feet, traded birdies at Nos. 10 and 11, respectively, before the U.S. broke through for good.

It was really only a matter of time.

"We get along well. We play fairly similar," Verplank said. "We grind it out pretty well, and we play

K.J. Choi had one birdie, at the third hole.

Second Day Four-ball Match 11

Geoff Ogilvy / Nick O'Hern

won 1 up over

Stewart Cink / Lucas Glover

Lucas Glover and Stewart Cink got off to a dream start in this one. It ended with a nightmare for Cink, and with the International Team of Geoff Ogilvy and Nick O'Hern accepting a late gift in a 1-up victory after a seesaw affair marked by spurts of great scoring.

With four 3s between them over the first four holes (one for Cink, at No. 2, and three for Glover), the Americans staked themselves to a quick 2-up lead on the Australian pair. However, Ogilvy and O'Hern were not about to shy away from the challenge thrown down.

Actually, it was O'Hern, the celebrated "Tiger killer," who was the first to respond with a series of key shots and once again showed his match-play mettle. The lefty rolled in a 12-footer at the sixth for birdie, then stuffed his next two approaches — 22 and 11 inches, respectively — to extend the birdie run to three straight for a 1-up International advantage.

Back came the Americans with three more birdies, but Ogilvy, coming off a bogey, trumped one of them at the par-5 12th when he chipped in from 40 feet for an eagle-3, canceling Glover's two-putt for a 4. Glover had squared it again at No. 10 when he made his fourth birdie of the day, this one from 15 feet.

Cink, who made few putts and needed 26 in 17 holes, not including concessions, finally got another on the board for the U.S. at No. 13 when he holed an 11-foot snake to once again square the proceedings.

It remained tied with a series of pars until the 17th, which spiraled into an ugly hole for the Americans. Glover's tee ball found the water, leaving Cink to battle the Aussies alone. His 52-foot birdie putt stopped two feet away. With his opponents safely in for par, Cink inexplicably rammed the second putt left. The Australians were handed a gift on a stroke that almost was short enough to be conceded.

"I came very close to giving it to him, but the greens were getting bumpy," admitted O'Hern, who avoided putting trouble by hitting at least a half-dozen shots inside eight feet. "I wasn't wishing him to miss, but that's match play."

After a great start, Lucas Glover and Stewart Cink faded.

Geoff Ogilvy's par at No. 14 kept the match tied.

Glover made the Internationals work for the win, as he birdied the final hole with a 10-foot putt. Ogilvy answered by caning his five-footer to halve the hole and lock up the victory. O'Hern, who hit 10 fairways and 14 greens, was the better player most of the day, but Ogilvy struck the winning blow and was just happy to pitch in here and there.

"We were down early on every hole, it seemed, and I just rode Nick all the way until I made one lucky birdie on the last hole," Ogilvy said with a grin. "That was my contribution. You know, it's just great fun. You just never know what's going to happen."

—*Dave Shedloski*

Nick O'Hern produced a series of key shots.

Second Day Four-ball Match 11																		
Hole	1	2	3	4	5	6	7	8	9	10	11	12	13	14	15	16	17	18
Par	4	4	4	4	3	5	3	4	4	4	4	5	3	4	4	4	3	4
Status	1 up	1 up	1 up	2 up	2 up	1 up	AS	-	-	AS	AS	-	AS	AS	AS	AS	-	-
Stewart Cink	4	3	4	4	3	5	3	4	4	-	5	4	2	5	4	4	4	4
Lucas Glover	3	-	3	3	3	5	3	4	5	3	4	4	3	4	4	4	-	3
Geoff Ogilvy	4	-	-	4	3	4	2	-	4	4	5	3	4	4	4	4	3	3
Nick O'Hern	4	3	3	5	3	4	2	3	4	4	4	4	3	4	4	4	3	4
Status	-	-	-	-	-	-	AS	1 up	1 up	AS	AS	1 up	AS	AS	AS	AS	1 up	1 up

Geoff Ogilvy and Nick O'Hern (International) defeated Stewart Cink and Lucas Glover (U.S.), 1 up.

Second Day Four-ball Match 12

Trevor Immelman / Rory Sabbatini
halved with

Woody Austin / David Toms

Woody Austin's 16-foot birdie on No. 17 squared the match.

Woody Austin started the day a 43-year-old Presidents Cup rookie with a wacky sense of humor and an often short fuse. At least when it came to his unruly putter.

He ended it a legend.

What transpired at the 14th hole Friday was a moment we'll never forget. One born from Austin listening to his caddie tell him he could get the errant shot out of the chilly water and onto the green, and of his foot on a slippery rock; one immediately perpetuated by ESPN and YouTube.

Yes, Austin listened to his caddie, Brent Henley, pulled on Henley's rain suit, peeled off his shoes and socks, and waded in. And no sooner than his club hit the water, he fell in. Popped right back up, but ... it wasn't long until they were calling him Aqua Man.

"By the time my head got out of the water, I was laughing," Austin said. "That's when I realized I was an idiot."

It's not often that someone is best remembered for something they never finished, but that's the case here. Austin and Toms took "X" on the hole. They

Second Day Four-ball Match 12																		
Hole	1	2	3	4	5	6	7	8	9	10	11	12	13	14	15	16	17	18
Par	4	4	4	4	3	5	3	4	4	4	4	5	3	4	4	4	3	4
Status	AS	1 up	AS	AS	-	-	AS	AS	1 up	AS	-	-	-	-	-	-	AS	AS
Woody Austin	4	3	4	4	3	-	2	3	3	4	5	4	3	-	4	3	2	3
David Toms	4	-	4	4	3	4	2	4	4	4	5	4	3	-	4	4	3	4
Trevor Immelman	4	4	3	4	3	-	-	4	4	3	4	4	4	-	4	4	3	4
Rory Sabbatini	4	4	5	4	2	4	3	3	4	4	4	4	3	-	4	4	3	3
Status	AS	-	AS	AS	1 up	1 up	AS	AS	-	AS	1 up	1 up	1 up	2 up	2 up	1 up	AS	AS

Woody Austin and David Toms (U.S.) halved with Trevor Immelman and Rory Sabbatini (International).

David Toms took a bogey-5 at No. 11.

Rory Sabbatini and Trevor Immelman celebrated the halve.

conceded the hole since both Immelman and Sabbatini were looking at birdie putts and both Americans had found the water.

"In retrospect, you could say that since (Toms) hit into the water, I should have laid up," Austin said. "But that's the reason the tee is up there, to get guys like Sabbatini and myself to go for it."

And, in Austin's case, go get it out of the water.

"The whole idea of the shot was just to try and get it to the bank, because I felt like from that bank, I had a chance to make 3," Austin said. "If I drop it from where I drop it, 30 yards over a little corner — at that point I knew deep down I probably couldn't pull off the shot. But between wanting really badly to pull it off and having my caddie urge me on ..."

But it's what happened next that's the real story. Austin shook off the water, the chants and everyone's jokes and birdied the next three holes to halve the match. Actually Austin carried the load most of the day, but he slid in a seven-footer at the 16th, a 16-foot birdie at the 17th to square the match, and hit his

approach stiff to six feet at the 18th for his fifth birdie of the match.

Austin took abuse the rest of the day — well, the first wave of it.

Vijay Singh walked by and said, "Woody, the Russian judge only gave you an 8 on that dive."

Austin couldn't stop laughing. Or joining in with a little self-deprecation, especially when Scott Verplank made sure reporters were looking when he sniffed Austin's damp collar.

"Well, I don't think I look any worse than I always do," Austin laughed. "Scotty says I smell different, but I think, you know, everything else, I think I look just as ugly as I always do."

But nothing was prettier than that halve.

—*Melanie Hauser*

Americans Dominate Foursomes

As much as they like their golf up in the Great White North, hockey is still king in Canada. And after Saturday's double round of match play at The Presidents Cup was complete, the International Team found itself needing nothing short of the kind of "Miracle on Ice" that lifted the United States to the 1980 Olympic gold medal.

"From our standpoint, it was a great day," U.S. Captain Jack Nicklaus said. "I couldn't be more pleased. Tomorrow, I don't want to take anything for granted. We have to win three points. We have to win three out of 12 matches. But they all start out the first hole even. So I want to make sure the guys tonight understand that we've got some work to do to get it done."

Nicklaus's International counterpart, Gary Player, was subdued as he pondered the uphill battle that lay ahead in Singles on Sunday. The eternal optimist in him, though, refused to lose hope. "I think — well, the odds are stacked up against us," he said. "But we saw some strange things happen at Brookline in the (1999) Ryder Cup the year Ben Crenshaw captained the (U.S.) Ryder Cup."

Not to mention, Player has experienced some strange things. He overcame a seven-stroke deficit to win the 1978 Masters, making birdie on seven of the final 10 holes to shoot 64 and win by a stroke. He didn't plan to conjure up images from the past and cajole his players to victory, though.

Phil Mickelson (opposite) and Woody Austin contributed to the U.S. sweep in Foursomes.

"I'm certainly not going in as an old poop and telling young guys, I did that, I did this, I did that," Player said. "They know these stories, so I'm certainly not going to blow my trumpet and tell them the time I came back. They know what they have to do. And I've always said this to my team: Play well. It doesn't matter who you play. ... I've always said to them, you expect every match to be tough.

"There ain't no such thing as an easy match. Go out there, if you play well, you win."

The Americans swept Saturday morning's Foursomes matches — giving the U.S. 10½ of the 11 points available in the alternate-shot format that once was its nemesis. The Internationals, at least, managed to keep pace in the afternoon Four-ball matches, but the 2½-to-2½ split left the U.S. with a commanding lead entering Sunday's Singles.

"This morning was amazing," Nicklaus said. "For us to win all five matches, I never dreamed that would happen. And to have us win 10½ out of 11 points in Foursomes, which we're not necessarily that good at, was pretty astounding for the two days."

Player and Captain's Assistant Ian Baker-Finch were at a loss to explain the International Team's ineptitude in Foursomes in this, the seventh renewal of The Presidents Cup. The Aussie assistant called the drubbing "shocking," while Ernie Els admitted the Americans appeared to have "rectified" what once was their Achilles heel.

"We put a lot of time in trying to select what we thought were really strong teams, good mates,

Retief Goosen teamed with Adam Scott for a halve in their Four-ball match.

that little ball doesn't know a damn thing about paper.

"So here I look at our team and yet America is beating us, on the overall series, they are beating us. Golf is a game of contradictions. It's a puzzle without an answer. And that's what makes it so great."

Only one Foursomes match reached the 18th hole on Saturday, so clear was the U.S. advantage. The Four-ball matches were a different story, though, as Phil Mickelson made birdie on the last to get a halve for himself and Woody Austin, while Stewart Cink had to birdie Nos. 16 and 17 to extend the match for a U.S. win.

"That was the turnaround, those two matches right there," Nicklaus said. "We don't win (and halve) those two matches, it's a different story going into tomorrow."

Cink, who sat out the morning's alternate-shot competition, said the Americans' success over the first three rounds of match play gave the U.S. Team a boost. "I think that when you have matches that come down to the very last hole or two, that swing in your favor, it tends to give you a lot of confidence next time you come down the last few holes when you're having a tight match," he said.

"It just gives you that sense of belief that you're going to be able to pull it out, and a lot of times you do. These matches are always so close between a team like theirs and a team like ours; that it almost always comes down to somebody just having that little bit of extra confidence at the end to pull it through."

Tiger Woods, who had absorbed his worst beating ever in team match play on Friday, came back strong with two wins on Saturday. He said the momentum swing was understandable. "We were up in all of the

good friends, like games, all of the things that you try and put together," Baker-Finch said. "Momentum is a huge thing in team sport, as these two (captains) know far better than me; that the momentum swing really went against us in those two things.

"And we can't really put our finger on any one thing, except a few guys that we had in place that are good putters didn't putt well this week, and really, if two of you are not putting well on a team, it's so hard to win. It's almost like dragging a dead weight behind you."

Player, for his part, refused to offer any excuses. The bottom line is the team that plays the best wins, he said.

"You know, you see remarkable things," Player explained. "To me, here, Europe is beating America in the Ryder Cup like a drum. I just look at it and then I look at our team and I say, well, you know, we've got a much better team than Europe on paper, but

matches and you feed off one another and you look on the board, it gives you energy, every time you see red, for us up on the board," he explained.

The Internationals would bank on Mike Weir, Canada's favorite son, to spark a comeback of Olympic proportions on Sunday. One of the unique aspects of The Presidents Cup is that the captains alternate match picks so there is a choice of opponents. When Nicklaus put Woods out in the fourth match, Player countered with Weir.

"If there's one player on our team that can really give Tiger a go, it will be Mike Weir," said Els, who partnered the diminutive Canadian to two Four-ball wins. "He's going to have all of Canada behind him tomorrow. I think it will be great for the tournament. I think it will be great for the fans, and for television, to have him go against Tiger."

—*Helen Ross*

Third Day

Morning Foursomes Matches

International	United States
0 Points	**5 Points**

Afternoon Four-ball Matches

International	United States
2½ Points	**2½ Points**

Third Day Total

International	United States
7½ Points	**14½ Points**

Third Day Foursomes Match 13

Steve Stricker / Hunter Mahan

won 2 up over

Trevor Immelman / Rory Sabbatini

The Americans, with Steve Stricker hitting from a bunker, lost the 17th hole but held on for a 2-up victory.

The International duo of Rory Sabbatini and Trevor Immelman wielded hot putters early on a cool, crisp morning in Saturday's opening Foursomes match, which is usually a recipe for success in team match play competition. Establish momentum and ride it out.

Not this time, however.

Steve Stricker found himself behind in a match for the first time in three sessions, but continual pressure by him and rookie teammate Hunter Mahan eventually wore down the South African pair in a 2-up triumph that ignited an American onslaught.

On back-to-back holes Sabbatini converted from 11 feet for birdie at No. 2 and Immelman drained a 26-foot birdie at No. 3 for a quick 2-up advantage.

But the Americans, playing steadily, got one back at the par-5 sixth. The Internationals needed four to reach the green and bogeyed, and they then conceded the U.S. birdie.

The key juncture came at the next hole, which the U.S. didn't win, but easily could have lost. Mahan blew his tee shot on the benign 153-yard par-3 over the green and to the left, and Stricker could only gouge the recovery out to about 20 feet. With the

South Africans in with a par, Mahan made up for his wayward approach by draining the putt to remain one back.

"After the sixth hole — we got one back there — we didn't want to lose any momentum and made a nice putt there and carried on from there," Mahan said. "We got off to a good start, hitting lots of fairways, and we kind of put some pressure on them. Kept putting the ball in play and in good position, and we had a good middle stretch there where we won a bunch of holes."

The payoff wasn't immediate, but the U.S. duo finally drew even at the 11th with a four-foot par putt. As they walked off the green, they traded knuckle bumps with Captain Jack Nicklaus, who had arrived to give them a charge.

Charge they did. Stricker stuck a wedge to two feet at the next for the first U.S. lead in the match. At the time, that win gave the Americans the lead in all five Foursomes matches.

Finally nosing ahead, the U.S. duo didn't let up. Stricker's 30-footer at No. 14 made it a 2-up advantage, and although they lost the 17th after missing the green and bogeying, the U.S. pair closed it out with a winning par for their second full point together. Stricker ran his record for the week to 3-0. Immelman lost for the fifth time since his debut match in 2005, and he and Sabbatini suffered their second straight disappointing result, having been the victim the previous day of Woody Austin's water-logged rally.

Rory Sabbatini and Trevor Immelman were ahead after 10 holes.

"We did well again today, Hunter and I. We teamed up well," Stricker said. "We needed to come out today and play well and make a bit of a statement. We knew we couldn't rest on our laurels."

—*Dave Shedloski*

Third Day Foursomes Match 13																		
Hole	1	2	3	4	5	6	7	8	9	10	11	12	13	14	15	16	17	18
Par	4	4	4	4	3	5	3	4	4	4	4	5	3	4	4	4	3	4
Status	AS	-	-	-	-	-	-	-	-	-	AS	1 up	1 up	2 up	2 up	2 up	1 up	2 up
Steve Stricker Hunter Mahan	4	4	4	4	3	C	3	4	4	4	4	4	3	3	4	4	-	4
Trevor Immelman Rory Sabbatini	4	3	3	4	3	-	3	4	4	4	5	5	3	4	4	4	C	5
Status	AS	1 up	2 up	2 up	2 up	1 up	1 up	1 up	1 up	1 up	AS	-	-	-	-	-	-	-

Steve Stricker and Hunter Mahan (U.S.) defeated Trevor Immelman and Rory Sabbatini (International), 2 up.

Third Day Foursomes Match 14

Phil Mickelson / Woody Austin

won 5 and 4 over

Retief Goosen / Stuart Appleby

Woody Austin got his first match victory.

This one was easier. Much easier.

Phil Mickelson and Woody Austin had collected a half-point in Foursomes on Thursday, ending an extremely hard-fought match that saw each team win six holes with the United States conceding Vijay Singh's 3½-foot putt on Royal Montreal's 18th. Two days later, the duo dusted their International counterparts, Retief Goosen and Stuart Appleby, 5 and 4 — sparking a rout that saw the Americans win all five matches.

The erratic Internationals actually were their own worst enemies, giving the U.S. the edge with three bogeys in a four-hole stretch. The Americans won the 10th hole when Mickelson chipped in from the right rough for birdie to go 3 up and gained even more of a cushion with an International bogey at No. 13.

Mickelson's clinching three-footer on the 14th hole turned out to be just the second birdie of the day for the game and opportunistic Americans. It was more than enough, though, to get the Americans rolling on their way to the thorough thrashing.

The win was the fiery Austin's first in his first

Third Day Foursomes Match 14																		
Hole	1	2	3	4	5	6	7	8	9	10	11	12	13	14	15	16	17	18
Par	4	4	4	4	3	5	3	4	4	4	4	5	3	4	4	4	3	4
Status	AS	AS	AS	AS	1 up	2 up	1 up	2 up	2 up	3 up	3 up	3 up	4 up	5 up				
Phil Mickelson Woody Austin	4	4	4	5	3	5	-	4	4	3	5	5	3	3				
Retief Goosen Stuart Appleby	4	4	4	5	4	6	C	5	4	4	5	5	4	4				
Status	AS	AS	AS	AS	-	-	-	-	-	-	-	-	-	-				

Phil Mickelson and Woody Austin (U.S.) defeated Retief Goosen and Stuart Appleby (International), 5 and 4.

Phil Mickelson had found a good partner.

Retief Goosen's team fell behind early.

Presidents Cup and he had now added two points to the U.S. cause, while Mickelson's record in three matches this year was 1-1-1. The veteran had a win and a halve with the rookie Austin, who made the highlight reel when he fell face-first into the lake after hitting a shot from the water at the 14th hole on Friday.

"This golf course is fun," Mickelson said. "We can make birdies on this course. And I had a great partner in 'Aqua Man.' He's a leader and I have enjoyed playing with him." Austin returned the compliment. "I said Thursday I can't play with a better person. We've cracked each other up for five days and I can't wait to do it again."

In Austin, Mickelson appeared to have found the same type of partnership he had with Chris DiMarco in the 2005 Presidents Cup. The two won all four of their matches that year, and Mickelson and Austin were off to a similarly solid start.

"An important element of the U.S. Team in The Presidents Cup and the Ryder Cup is having young, youthful rookies," Mickelson said. "I wouldn't say rookies, but (players who) actually haven't played in any team events, because Woody Austin, Hunter Mahan, they bring an exuberance to this event, and it feeds off of us.

"We end up playing these team events now every year, and have since '94, and to have guys like Woody and Hunter to remind us of how fun it is and exciting it is (is good). Not that we were not excited, but it really gets us focused and excited to play. We work well together because I'm able to maybe provide a little bit of stability and he's able to provide some excitement. We really work well together."

—*Helen Ross*

Third Day Foursomes Match 15

Tiger Woods / Jim Furyk
won 4 and 3 over
Adam Scott / Ernie Els

Following the worst team match loss of his career, Tiger Woods was paired with Jim Furyk in a 4-and-3 Foursomes romp.

Jim Furyk was still shaking his head over Friday's loss. No way to explain it.

No reason to belabor it, either. Not after what he and Tiger Woods had just done.

In a bounce-back of world-class proportions, Furyk and Woods went from a Four-ball loss — the biggest in Woods's career — to a 4-and-3 Foursomes romp over heavyweights Adam Scott and Ernie Els.

"It was nice to come out, I think sometimes that puts a little fire under your rear end," Furyk said.

It showed. Els and Scott, who teamed for two Foursomes points at the 2003 Presidents Cup, stumbled at the first hole and never really seemed to recover. They were out of sync and ice cold on the greens — they missed a combined five birdie putts inside 19 feet. Definitely not the combination you want facing America's top team.

The Americans were impressive with putts fall-

Jim Furyk felt a 'fire' in the match.

ing at all the right times. They jumped to a 2-up lead after three holes and birdied five holes to one for the Internationals. And, they made this look stress-free. But it wasn't.

"We went out there and made some birdies," Woods said. "Adam and Ernie had opportunities to make putts on the front nine and get to all-square, but just didn't make the putts."

Tiger's 24-foot birdie gave the U.S. a 2-up lead at the third hole, but the Americans bogeyed the next to drop a hole. And Els is still shaking his head at the fifth hole where his 10-footer lipped out when he was trying to match Furyk's 14-foot birdie that kept the Americans 2 up.

The Internationals struggled to keep up and did until Furyk's bunker shot at the 12th gave Tiger a nine-foot putt to go 3 up. After Els's tee shot found the water at the 14th, Scott came an inch away from holing the next shot. It didn't matter as Furyk slid in

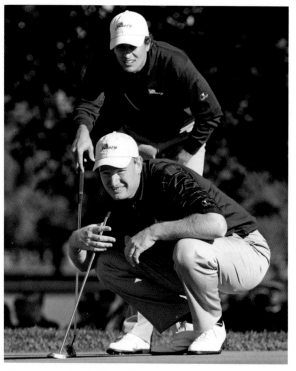

Adam Scott and Ernie Els couldn't keep pace.

a 3½-footer to give the Americans a 4-up lead with four holes to play.

Els was loose on the second shot at No. 15, Tiger came up a roll short on his birdie putt, and the match ended with a pair of pars.

"They had their opportunities, but couldn't get the putts to fall," Furyk said.

—*Melanie Hauser*

Third Day Foursomes Match 15																		
Hole	1	2	3	4	5	6	7	8	9	10	11	12	13	14	15	16	17	18
Par	4	4	4	4	3	5	3	4	4	4	4	5	3	4	4	4	3	4
Status	1 up	1 up	2 up	1 up	2 up	2 up	2 up	2 up	2 up	2 up	2 up	2 up	3 up	3 up	4 up	4 up		
Tiger Woods Jim Furyk	4	4	3	5	2	5	2	4	4	4	4	4	3	3	4			
Adam Scott Ernie Els	5	4	4	4	3	5	2	4	4	4	4	5	3	4	4			
Status	-	-	-	-	-	-	-	-	-	-	-	-	-	-	-			

Tiger Woods and Jim Furyk (U.S.) defeated Adam Scott and Ernie Els (International), 4 and 3.

Third Day Foursomes Match 16

Lucas Glover / Scott Verplank
won 2 and 1 over
Vijay Singh / Mike Weir

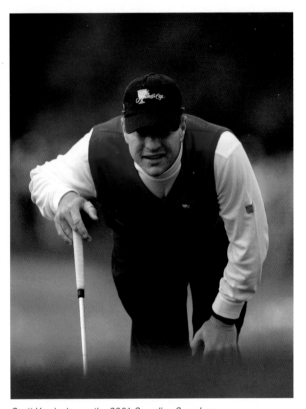

Scott Verplank won the 2001 Canadian Open here.

Scott Verplank loves a good fight. So when he and Lucas Glover drew Canada's favorite son Mike Weir and red-hot Vijay Singh in Saturday morning's Foursomes ... well, his first thought was bring it on.

"You know they are going to be tough and they are both going to play hard," Verplank said. "I was looking forward to a chance to play with Mike Weir because I knew the crowd would be so good and really supportive of him."

Make that boisterous. Or over-the-top. Biggest and loudest crowd of the day, complete wth a group of fans dressed in white caddie jumpsuits with "Weir" written on the backs.

On any other day, the fans might have been pulling for Verplank, who won the 2001 Canadian Open at Royal Montreal. That, of course, makes him an instant favorite.

But not Saturday. Not with The Presidents Cup on the line and Glover beside him.

America's new go-to pair had knocked off Retief Goosen and Stuart Appleby in Thursday's opening Foursomes, which simply made their chemistry

Third Day Foursomes Match 16																		
Hole	1	2	3	4	5	6	7	8	9	10	11	12	13	14	15	16	17	18
Par	4	4	4	4	3	5	3	4	4	4	4	5	3	4	4	4	3	4
Status	-	AS	AS	AS	-	-	AS	-	AS	1 up	1 up	2 up	2 up	3 up	2 up	2 up	2 up	
Lucas Glover Scott Verplank	5	3	4	5	4	5	2	4	3	3	5	4	3	3	4	4	3	
Vijay Singh Mike Weir	4	4	4	5	3	5	3	3	4	4	5	5	3	4	3	4	3	
Status	1 up	AS	AS	AS	1 up	1 up	AS	1 up	AS	-	-	-	-	-	-	-	-	

Lucas Glover and Scott Verplank (U.S.) defeated Vijay Singh and Mike Weir (International), 2 and 1.

Many would have caddied for their Canadian hero.

Mike Weir's pitch at the fifth yielded a brief lead.

even stronger. Singh and Weir, on the other hand, had halved their opening Foursomes match with Phil Mickelson and Woody Austin.

In this one, the International Team opened with a par to go 1 up, but the Americans came right back to even the match at the second hole. Neither team was sharp early, but Verplank got things going with close approaches, including one to nine feet at the seventh hole, and Glover started rolling them in.

Singh, the only International player to compete in every Presidents Cup, missed a short one at the ninth hole to allow the U.S. to square the match, and the Americans responded with yet another back-nine wake-up call at the 10th. They went up for good there with a birdie to start a three-birdies-in-five-holes stretch. Verplank added a birdie at the 12th, then hit it stiff at the 14th to give the U.S. a 3-up lead.

Singh found a little of his Friday magic — he holed out from just off the green on the 15th hole — but it was too little, too late. Weir's birdie try at the 16th was just off, and the match ended at No. 17 with a pair of pars.

The Americans did their best to take the crowd out of it with Verplank's iron shots, a pair of bunker saves from Glover and Glover's putting, but the Canadian crowd made it tough until the end.

"It made it more fun to be honest with you," Verplank said.

And for a better fight. What more could he ask?

With Lucas Glover hitting to the green, the U.S. won the ninth.

Perhaps for Glover as a permanent Foursomes partner.

"We're very comfortable," Verplank said. "I think that a big part of it is getting comfortable with your partner and having fun."

—Melanie Hauser

51

Third Day Foursomes Match 17

Zach Johnson / David Toms

won 2 and 1 over

Nick O'Hern / Geoff Ogilvy

Geoff Ogilvy drove to square the match at No. 14.

America completed an inexplicable but impressive sweep of the Saturday morning Foursomes when David Toms, continuing his unbeaten run in Montreal, teamed with Zach Johnson to convert six birdies and dispatch resilient Nick O'Hern and Geoff Ogilvy, 2 and 1.

The Americans were thoroughly in control of the match when Toms converted at 12-footer for birdie at the 10th and a 3-up lead, but the proceedings started out with the Aussies securing the advantage — only to give it back. The U.S. pair jumped on the opening.

O'Hern's wedge to three feet on the second hole set up an easy birdie for Ogilvy that put the pair ahead. But bunkered at the par-3 fifth, Ogilvy left the second shot in the trap and the Aussies had to con-

cede the hole because Toms was sizing up a five-footer for birdie.

So much for momentum.

So much momentum for the U.S. to build on. And they did.

On the sixth, Toms nailed another approach inside his shadow, and set up Johnson with an 11-footer at the seventh. The Masters champion buried that for the 2-up American lead.

The rout was on with Toms's birdie at the 10th, but there was no quit in the Aussies. They captured three of the next four holes to square the match on No. 14 with a little help from the U.S. duo, who bogeyed the 11th. O'Hern found the green at the par-5 12th with his second shot for a two-putt birdie, and then the lefty capped the rally with a chip-in birdie from the left rough at the 14th.

Now it was the U.S. sweating.

"We had all the momentum early through 10 holes and we gave one back at 11 and they birdied 12 and chipped in at 14," Toms said in assessing the situation. "We needed something good to happen, and we did that, and we just played solid holes after that and put pressure on them."

On No. 15, following a beautiful approach by Johnson to eight feet, Toms rolled in the go-ahead birdie putt. After solid pars by both at No. 16, the U.S. was conceded the match with a par on the 17th hole after the Aussies missed the green and then O'Hern failed to convert a six-foot par putt that would have pushed the match to No. 18.

"Zach and I had a great time this morning," said Toms, who had trailed for a total of four holes in his three matches thus far. "He played really well, gave

Zach Johnson believed in momentum.

a couple back on the back nine, and they had the momentum until we chipped in on 15. It was a good day and I knew our team was playing well. It was a lot quieter out here today and we can feed off that, and it was nice to get a point."

It was the final point of an American clean sweep in Foursomes, in fact.

Johnson just shrugged. "It's just a matter of getting some momentum, and that's the beauty of team match play," he said.

—*Dave Shedloski*

David Toms had trailed for only four holes.

Third Day Foursomes Match 17

Hole	1	2	3	4	5	6	7	8	9	10	11	12	13	14	15	16	17	18
Par	4	4	4	4	3	5	3	4	4	4	4	5	3	4	4	4	3	4
Status	AS	-	-	-	AS	1 up	2 up	2 up	2 up	3 up	2 up	1 up	1 up	AS	1 up	1 up	2 up	
Zach Johnson David Toms	4	4	4	4	C	4	2	4	4	3	5	5	3	3	3	4	3	
Nick O'Hern Geoff Ogilvy	4	3	4	4	-	5	3	4	4	4	4	4	3	2	4	4	4	
Status	AS	1 up	1 up	1 up	AS	-	-	-	-	-	-	-	-	AS	-	-	-	

Zach Johnson and David Toms (U.S.) defeated Nick O'Hern and Geoff Ogilvy (International), 2 and 1.

Third Day Four-ball Match 18

Stewart Cink / Jim Furyk
won 1 up over

Angel Cabrera / K.J. Choi

Stewart Cink, along with Jim Furyk, rallied to win.

Stewart Cink wasn't looking for redemption.

No, Cink wasn't pleased with himself for missing that 3½-foot putt Friday at the 17th hole — the little 160-yard par-3 with a lake just to the right of the green. The miss put him and Lucas Glover 1 down and cost them a halve.

But when Cink faced a seven-footer at the same hole Saturday, all he could think about was getting the putt to drop for the lead and another point. Not redemption.

"No, it didn't have anything to do with yesterday," said Cink, who birdied Nos. 14, 16 and 17. "It's golf and it happens, and I wish it had not happened, but it did. You just can't dwell on that kind of thing. … You move on and wait for your better days."

When Cink's putt hit the bottom of the cup, it marked yet another comeback for an American duo. Cink and Furyk were 2 down through the first 12 holes before rallying to win 1 up.

Of the four players, only Furyk had played in the morning matches. Both Cabrera and Choi seemed

Hole	1	2	3	4	5	6	7	8	9	10	11	12	13	14	15	16	17	18
Par	4	4	4	4	3	5	3	4	4	4	4	5	3	4	4	4	3	4
Status	1 up	1 up	2 up	2 up	2 up	1 up	AS	AS	-	-	-	-	-	-	-	AS	1 up	1 up
Stewart Cink	4	4	3	5	-	5	3	3	4	4	5	4	-	3	4	3	2	4
Jim Furyk	3	3	4	4	3	5	3	-	4	4	5	4	2	4	4	4	-	4
Angel Cabrera	4	3	4	4	-	4	3	4	3	4	5	4	3	3	4	4	3	4
K.J. Choi	4	4	4	4	3	-	2	3	4	3	5	4	3	4	4	4	3	4
Status	-	-	-	-	-	-	AS	AS	1 up	2 up	2 up	2 up	1 up	1 up	1 up	AS	-	-

Stewart Cink and Jim Furyk (U.S.) defeated Angel Cabrera and K.J. Choi (International), 1 up.

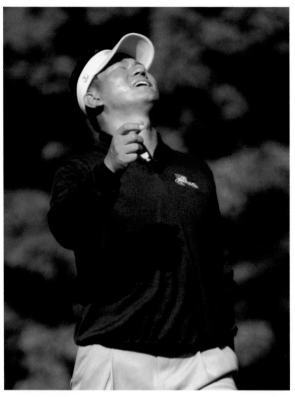

Cabrera posted birdies on the 13th and 14th holes.

K.J. Choi (above) and Angel Cabrera missed putts on No. 18.

tentative after sitting out the Foursomes, while Furyk slipped in a five-footer for birdie at the first hole and Cink dropped one at the third to give the Americans a 2-up lead after three holes. Then things turned.

Cink lipped out a birdie attempt at the sixth, while the Internationals birdied the sixth and seventh to square the match. After Cink and Choi sank long birdies at the eighth, Cabrera put his team 1 up with an approach that finished five feet from the hole at No. 9.

Choi scrambled for a birdie to put his team 2 up at the 10th, then, after Cabrera missed a six-footer that would have given the Internationals a 3-up lead, Furyk had a premonition. Something good was about to happen, he told Cink. And it did. He dropped a 32-footer at the 13th hole to cut the lead to 1 up.

Cink and Cabrera both birdied the 14th, then Cink sank a 15-foot birdie to square the match on the

16th hole. Then came his 9-iron to seven feet at No. 17. It was his fourth birdie in six holes and put the U.S. dormie going to No. 18.

"I didn't even see it as a run," Cink said. "I was trying to do my best on every shot and luckily some of my putts were for birdie. It felt good to escape from being in the jaws of defeat there."

Cabrera and Choi both missed birdie putts at the 18th to give the Americans their first point of the afternoon session.

"We finished strong," Furyk said. "My partner, you know, birdied 16 and 17 to flip a 1 down to 1 up, and we were able to hold on. It was a big point for the team. At one time today, it looked like we were definitely going to lose this section of the matches."

But their point sparked another U.S. run.

"I don't think we sensed that our point was any more important than the others, but having the first match come down to the wire and us end up on top, the way it happened, I think that sent a message out to the rest of the guys, and everybody pulled it really strong on the back nine." Cink said. "It means a lot for us to lead the team in that way."

—*Melanie Hauser*

Third Day Four-ball Match 19

Adam Scott / Retief Goosen
halved with
Phil Mickelson / Woody Austin

Aqua Man made a brief appearance. But he didn't wade into the water. His partner did.

When Woody Austin — aka Aqua Man after Friday's stumble in the water at the 14th hole — missed an eight-footer at the 15th, Phil Mickelson decided to try and play his shot out of the water. This was, after all, a tight match and the U.S. didn't need to go 1 down with three to play.

So Mickelson pulled on his rain gear and borrowed the left tennis shoe from caddie Jim Mackay and went in. The 14 extra wide was a bit big on Mickelson's size 13 foot, but it worked. Mickelson hit the shot, flubbed it, made a great recovery and, well, the U.S. still lost the hole as Adam Scott buried a 15-foot putt for birdie.

And no, he didn't think about flopping into the water.

"Did I think about swimming and trying to catch fish? No, I was just trying to hit a golf shot," Mickelson said. "But certainly Woody would have done it a little differently I think."

And his caddie wouldn't have been wearing a soggy shoe.

"He said later it was a roomy fit," Mackay said of the loaner shoe. "It's all about comfort. I didn't want him squishing down the 16th hole."

Adam Scott first squared the match with his birdie-2 on the seventh hole.

On No. 16, Retief Goosen holed a 68-foot bunker shot.

Phil Mickelson played from the water on No. 15.

That hole, it turned out, belonged to Goosen. The quiet South African holed a 68-foot bunker shot to pad the lead to 2 up, then America's good-time guys roared back. Austin made a clutch nine-foot putt at the 17th to extend the match, then Mickelson — with a read from Austin's putt — grabbed a halve with a 20-footer at the 18th.

"It was fun to birdie the last hole," Mickelson said. "It was fun to push that match when we were 2 down. It was fun the way Woody responded on 17 with that birdie, and right after Retief made the incredible bunker shot. It's fun to keep fighting when things don't look good. It looked like the match was over and we fought hard and were able to get a halve out of it."

Fun? This one was a deep sigh. And it was work.

This duo had the match, then they didn't. Then they did. Then they got a huge halve.

The Americans took a quick 1-up lead when Mickelson birdied from four feet at the second and held it until Scott squared the match with a three-footer at the seventh. The lead seesawed again, with Scott squaring the match at the 12th.

And, Austin, who was dogged all day with Aqua Man quips, had the chance to reprise his Friday flop into the water at No. 14 when his drive wound up in the lake again.

"He had numerous offers to increase his wealth if he would jump in the lake and go after his ball on 14, but he decided not to," Mickelson laughed.

—Melanie Hauser

Third Day Four-ball Match 19																		
Hole	1	2	3	4	5	6	7	8	9	10	11	12	13	14	15	16	17	18
Par	4	4	4	4	3	5	3	4	4	4	4	5	3	4	4	4	3	4
Status	AS	1 up	1 up	1 up	1 up	1 up	AS	1 up	AS	1 up	1 up	AS	AS	AS	-	-	-	AS
Phil Mickelson	4	3	4	-	3	5	3	3	4	3	-	5	4	3	5	4	-	3
Woody Austin	4	-	4	4	-	5	3	-	4	4	4	5	3	-	5	4	2	4
Adam Scott	4	4	4	4	3	5	2	4	4	4	4	4	3	3	4	-	3	4
Retief Goosen	4	-	4	4	3	5	3	4	3	4	4	-	3	-	4	3	3	5
Status	AS	-	-	-	-	-	AS	-	AS	-	-	AS	AS	AS	1 up	2 up	1 up	AS

Phil Mickelson and Woody Austin (U.S.) halved with Adam Scott and Retief Goosen (International).

Third Day Four-ball Match 20

Mike Weir / Ernie Els
won 4 and 2 over

Charles Howell III / Lucas Glover

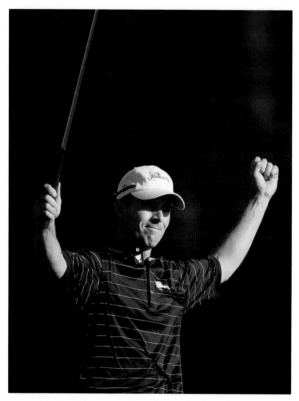

Mike Weir's 25-footer on No. 15 put the Internationals 3 up.

In three previous Presidents Cup appearances, Mike Weir and Ernie Els had never played together. Judging by their performance at Royal Montreal, though, future International Team captains might want to include this duo among their go-to teams.

The two couldn't be more different in stature — with Weir giving up six inches and nearly 50 pounds to the big South African — or style of play. But in Four-ball competition, the two were a potent combination, producing a pair of wins for the Internationals.

"I think I did find a new teammate in this format," Weir said. "We gelled well together, me being consistent and getting it in play and he can be aggressive on the par-5s and he drives the green on 14; that strategy works well."

Els set the tone for the match when he made birdie on the first hole. Lucas Glover, who was playing in his first Presidents Cup, answered at the second when he holed a shot for eagle, but the veteran from Johannesburg made birdie at No. 3 and the International Team began to take command.

Weir delighted the home crowd with a string of

Third Day Four-ball Match 20																		
Hole	1	2	3	4	5	6	7	8	9	10	11	12	13	14	15	16	17	18
Par	4	4	4	4	3	5	3	4	4	4	4	5	3	4	4	4	3	4
Status	-	AS	-	-	-	-	-	-	-	-	-	-	-	-	-	-		
Charles Howell III	5	-	4	4	-	-	3	4	4	-	4	5	3	3	4	-		
Lucas Glover	4	2	4	5	2	4	2	4	4	3	3	5	4	3	4	-		
Mike Weir	4	-	4	4	-	5	2	3	3	4	4	5	3	3	3	-		
Ernie Els	3	-	3	4	2	4	3	4	4	4	-	4	3	-	-	-		
Status	1 up	AS	1 up	1 up	1 up	1 up	1 up	2 up	3 up	2 up	1 up	2 up	2 up	2 up	3 up	4 up		

Mike Weir and Ernie Els (International) defeated Charles Howell III and Lucas Glover (U.S.), 4 and 2.

Ernie Els set the tone with birdies on Nos. 1 and 3.

Lucas Glover's round included an eagle at No. 2.

three straight birdies that began at No. 7 — the first to halve and the next two to put the Internationals 3 up. Glover responded with consecutive 10-footers for birdie at Nos. 10 and 11, but Els gave the Internationals some breathing room with a 10-footer to win the 12th and return to 2 up.

When he made a 25-footer for birdie at the 15th hole to earn a halve, Weir celebrated by thrusting both arms — and his putter — into the air as if to lead the cheers of the crowd. Els was staring at a five-footer and Weir had a birdie putt from 13 feet when the Americans conceded the match at the 16th hole.

The Internationals were 12 under and won for the second time in Four-ball during the week. "We had a lot of fun," Els said. "Mike obviously is the local man. They were shouting, 'Mike Weir for president.' I don't know how they elect presidents or prime ministers here but I think he's in the running, because

he has about 45,000 fans out there. He played wonderful, very steady. I had a great time."

Glover did his best to turn the tide, though. The Captain's Pick made 12 birdies and an eagle in 34 holes of Four-ball, although the former Clemson All-American came up empty in both matches.

"We had a good day," Els said. "Mike and myself, we were 12 under when we finished at 16. So we made a lot of birdies out there. ... We shot 28 on the front and we were only 3 up because Lucas, he was hanging in there. He even birdied 10 and 11 on the back, took us back to 1 up. I birdied 12, went back to 2 up.

"Then Mike made two great birdies on 14 and 15, and then obviously on 16, we were 3 up and I hit a good 5-iron in there. So that was the end of the match."

—Helen Ross

Third Day Four-ball Match 21

Vijay Singh / Stuart Appleby
won 1 up over
Steve Stricker / Hunter Mahan

Australian standout Stuart Appleby continued to put his struggles in past Presidents Cups behind him on Saturday afternoon with another strong performance with Vijay Singh in Four-ball action to give a lift to the International Team, which was still smarting from its Foursomes struggles.

Appleby, who despite eight PGA TOUR titles had entered this Presidents Cup with a meager 3-11-2 record, had teamed with Singh in a runaway victory over Tiger Woods and Jim Furyk on Friday. The International twosome seemed to pick up where they left off, holding the lead throughout and getting the bet-

Stuart Appleby 'got the job done' for a match victory.

ter of previously unbeaten Steve Stricker and Hunter Mahan in a 1-up decision.

"We got the job done," said Appleby, who improved to 4-3 in Four-ball. "We had it turned at 3 and really just went a little bit … petered out a little bit into the back nine, and they sort of made a bit of a run late. And Vijay had some good up-and-downs. I think we combined pretty well generally, just not as dynamic as the day before, so we squeezed it out down 18."

The Internationals, undoubtedly feeling some urgency, wasted no time jumping out front. Singh, who played sensational golf throughout the week, sank a four-foot birdie putt on the second hole for a 1-up lead.

The home squad could very well have been 2 up, but Stricker canceled Appleby's par at the long par-4 fourth hole (after both Americans had made a mess of it) by holing a difficult chip from the rough that had to negotiate 55 feet before finding the cup.

Appleby's two-putt birdie at the par-5 sixth hole made up for that missed opportunity, and both International players birdied the ninth for a 3-up advantage.

The Americans awakened at the 12th when Stricker converted a five-foot birdie putt. His six-footer at the 17th for birdie resulted in another U.S. win and pushed the match to the par-4 home hole.

Reeling a bit, the International pair both missed the fairway and the green. With the Americans already in with a par, Singh faced a five-footer to halve the hole and preserve the full point. He calmly guided it in and improved his record to 2-2 for the week and to 8-5-1 in Four-ball action.

Hunter Mahan contributed two birdies.

Appleby, who had not yet won a Singles match in his four previous Presidents Cup efforts, wasn't necessarily troubled by seeing the match go the distance, even if it did mean extra work and some heartache.

"It was good for me to play the last few holes I guess, because I had not seen many of the last few holes the days previous," Appleby said. "Good victory, and I've seemed to struggle to find wins, and at least I got a couple this week. If I can squeak out a win tomorrow that would be great, because I haven't had one yet, and, obviously, more than a few of us have to get wins tomorrow.

Vijay Singh and Steve Stricker were the more experienced partners.

"We need three to five horses out of the gate quick," he added. "We need ups and we need wins. There is no backing up. That is our hurdle."

—Dave Shedloski

Third Day Four-ball Match 21																		
Hole	1	2	3	4	5	6	7	8	9	10	11	12	13	14	15	16	17	18
Par	4	4	4	4	3	5	3	4	4	4	4	5	3	4	4	4	3	4
Status	AS	-	-	-	-	-	-	-	-	-	-	-	-	-	-	-	-	-
Steve Stricker	4	4	4	4	3	5	3	3	4	4	4	4	3	-	4	4	2	4
Hunter Mahan	5	4	3	-	3	5	3	-	-	4	-	5	-	3	-	4	-	4
Vijay Singh	4	3	4	4	3	5	3	4	3	4	4	5	3	3	-	4	-	4
Stuart Appleby	4	4	3	4	3	4	3	3	3	4	4	5	3	4	4	4	3	5
Status	AS	1 up	1 up	1 up	1 up	2 up	2 up	2 up	3 up	3 up	3 up	2 up	2 up	2 up	2 up	2 up	1 up	1 up

Vijay Singh and Stuart Appleby (International) defeated Steve Stricker and Hunter Mahan (U.S.), 1 up.

Third Day Four-ball Match 22

Tiger Woods / David Toms

won 5 and 3 over

Nick O'Hern / Geoff Ogilvy

David Toms had played on several Presidents Cup and Ryder Cup teams with Tiger Woods, but had never been partnered with the No. 1 player in the world. His request to get one chance to join Woods was fulfilled by Captain Jack Nicklaus.

The Americans fulfilled their duty of adding another point to the overall tally.

Nick O'Hern and Geoff Ogilvy had little chance in this one. Toms was brilliant early and then Woods piled on later and even a late kick did little to puncture the Yanks' confidence as they rolled to a 5-and-3 decision in Saturday's final match.

The Americans combined to shoot nine-under par in the Four-ball format to register an overwhelming victory one day after Woods was on the losing end of an almost similar decision. But Woods let Toms do some of the heavy lifting early and the Louisianan was up to the task, making three birdies in the first six holes as the U.S. duo surged ahead 2 up.

Toms got rolling at No. 2 with a laser wedge from 116 yards that stopped inches from the hole for a conceded birdie. Woods, after a 323-yard drive, knocked

Driving on No. 14, David Toms birdied to be 4 up.

Third Day Four-ball Match 22																		
Hole	1	2	3	4	5	6	7	8	9	10	11	12	13	14	15	16	17	18
Par	4	4	4	4	3	5	3	4	4	4	4	5	3	4	4	4	3	4
Status	AS	1 up	2 up	2 up	2 up	2 up	2 up	3 up	4 up	4 up	3 up	3 up	3 up	4 up	5 up			
Tiger Woods	4	4	-	4	3	4	3	3	3	4	4	4	3	-	3			
David Toms	-	3	3	4	3	-	3	-	4	4	4	-	2	3	-			
Nick O'Hern	4	4	4	5	3	4	3	4	4	4	4	4	2	-	-			
Geoff Ogilvy	4	4	4	4	3	-	3	4	4	4	3	-	-	4	4			
Status	AS	-	-	-	-	-	-	-	-	-	-	-	-	-	-			

David Toms and Tiger Woods (U.S.) defeated Nick O'Hern and Geoff Ogilvy (Interntional), 5 and 3.

Nick O'Hern was swamped by the Americans.

a wedge to 10 feet at the third hole and drained it, and the U.S. pair never really looked back. Toms canceled the Aussie's first birdie with his own at the sixth to preserve the advantage.

Woods missed the green at the eighth, but that hardly has bothered him with his chipping game. Lo and behold, he bumped the ball cleanly into the cup from 30 feet for birdie. O'Hern couldn't answer from nine feet, a huge deflator when it looked as if the Internationals might pick up a hole instead of fall farther back.

Smelling blood in the water, Woods then followed with another wonderfully judged wedge to five feet at No. 9 and buried that for birdie to increase the lead to four.

Ogilvy finally got a putt to drop at No. 11, sinking a 12-footer to ignite a run of three straight birdies. At the 12th, O'Hern dropped a wedge to within inches only to watch Woods's power cancel him out. Woods ripped a 3-wood from 262 yards that stopped within 10 feet of the hole for an easy two-putt birdie and a halve.

When Toms converted a five-footer at No. 14, the Americans went dormie. For good measure, Woods strafed the Internationals with a 42-footer for birdie to end it with an exclamation point.

Toms finished the matches 4-0-1, making him the leading scorer for the American side.

Tiger Woods holed a 42-foot winning putt.

"I had some good partners," Toms demurred with his usual modest manner. "First time I got to play with Tiger. I guess this is my sixth international competition in a row, and I've yet to play with him until this week, so that was a lot of fun. There are a lot of things I'll take from this week, a lot of new partners, a lot of good times. You know, I was just lucky enough to contribute to the team."

—Dave Shedloski

U.S. Team, Weir Share Accolades

Go ahead. Call him a sentimental old fool — Jack Nicklaus isn't about to argue with you. And Sunday's 19½ to 14½ United States victory over the Internationals in the seventh Presidents Cup will forever be one of those "special moments" in a life chock full of the kind that made time stand still, a life that has seen Nicklaus set the standards to which every golfer aspires.

In the last three renewals of this spirited biennial competition, Nicklaus and International Captain Gary Player have set a tone for The Presidents Cup that emphasizes sportsmanship while also showcasing players at the top of their game — and what unfolded at Royal Montreal was no exception. The victory was the second straight for the U.S. after that landmark tie in South Africa in 2003.

Nicklaus, though, doesn't dwell on his more-than-respectable 2-1-1 record as the American captain. He prefers to focus on the relationships he's formed with players on both teams, but most of all with the Americans he's captained and their families. Clearly moved by Sunday's victory, Nicklaus, who said he had a "blast" in 2007, struggled to maintain his composure during the closing ceremonies.

"You get wrapped up in 12 guys' lives, and you're trying to not only lead them, but also make sure that their wives are part of what's going on, and that they are part of the team," Nicklaus said later. "It's all

Tiger Woods said Mike Weir (both opposite) had a 'phenomenal' week after Weir won in the Singles.

very special and I get very sentimental about it. I'm sentimental about it right now. I know that as you get older, you're right, your years are shorter; that you may not have those opportunities again.

"It may be the last time that I do it. And if that's the case, that's fine. That's a pretty good way to bow out. You know, the reaction that I get from these guys and the support that I've gotten from them, not only the support that I've tried to give them, but the support they have given me, is just something that you don't have very many times in a lifetime."

Nicklaus said he didn't want to be "piggish" but he left open the possibility that he might return for the matches in 2009 at Harding Park Golf Course in San Francisco. While Player maintained it was "time" to yield to another captain, his players — particularly Vijay Singh — made it clear they'd like another shot with the Black Knight at the helm.

"I've got more of these than anybody else out here," said the big man from Fiji, holding up the consolation medal. "We had a great team on paper. We are just much stronger than the American team but we just didn't have it in the Foursomes. I don't know why. We had great combinations, but we just didn't do it.

"Going out today, I was telling Gary, I think he gave one of the most inspirational speeches that I've ever heard. ... I think we had everything going, but we just were too far behind. Hopefully I'm in the team in two years' time, and maybe we can do it in San Francisco. I think that's our goal, and hopefully

Weir approached No. 18 on the way to victory.

Gary Player praised both teams.

Gary is our captain again and we can do it for him."

The U.S. won five of Sunday's 12 Singles matches to seal the victory, which was its fifth against one loss and the historic tie at Fancourt. The Americans more than paved the way to the title, though, with a stellar performance in Foursomes — winning 10½ of the 11 available points on Thursday and Saturday morning.

The International Team made a spirited bid on Sunday, but it simply had dug too big a hole entering the mano-y-mano phase of the competition. The seven Singles wins — which included Mike Weir's 1-up win over Tiger Woods, much to the delight of his countrymen — were more than the International Team had ever put together, but hardly enough to turn back the Americans.

"I could hear the roar and stuff, and watching the scoreboard all day," said Els, who was playing two matches ahead of Weir and Woods. "It must have lifted the whole team, really. That's what we were looking for, and obviously we needed early matches. But again, it was only going to be a miracle for us to win this thing.

"But I think the guys played really well today. As Gary mentioned, we're 7-5 in this session. We won both Four-ball sessions. The only thing, we got trounced in the Foursomes sessions. … It's almost like a test match, a cricket match. You have your sessions, and we just had two bad ones. They scored about a thousand runs against us in those two, if you take it into a cricket match.

"But I think we did okay today. The guys showed a lot of guts today and played well."

Weir, who had started the competition as somewhat of a controversial Captain's Pick, showed Player's confidence in him was well-placed. He went 3-1-1 overall — only Els, his partner in two Four-ball wins, had as many victories for the Internationals at Royal Montreal — and Weir did his part on Sunday by rallying to beat Woods. The Americans had simply built too large a lead, a "monumental hill," as Player would later say.

"I think Gary just believed in the way I was playing this week and I believed in the way I was playing," said Weir, who was 3 up through 10 holes against

Woods only to find himself 1 down five holes later. "We needed some motivation being down so much. We thought if maybe I could possibly get off to a really good start and see me doing some good stuff today, that would maybe spur on the rest of the guys. So that was really the strategy behind that."

Weir called the support from the raucous Canadian fans "overwhelming, really," and allowed that when he looked back on his career, the love he felt from those fans was "maybe even more special" than his Masters victory. As he congratulated Weir for the job well done, Player said the win would be a "big thing" in the 2003 Masters champion's life.

Jack Nicklaus described his experience: 'Something that you don't have very many times in a lifetime.'

"I felt good about my game today," Weir said. "I just kind of expected anything today. I just felt like I was just prepared for anything. Even though when I got up early on Tiger, not that I was hoping he would make a comeback, but I was just prepared for when that happened; so when it did happen, I didn't panic."

Indeed. Weir calmly rolled in a 10-footer at the 17th hole to extend the match and won the point when Woods could not hole a chip after hitting his tee shot into the hazard at No. 18. "Can you imagine the pressure for him on the last hole? And he didn't back off, he banged it right at the flag. And in front of your own people, this will turn his life around," Player said.

"For the pressure that he had all week, it was pretty phenomenal how he had to deal with that and the way he played," Woods said. "I mean, not a lot of people could actually have dealt with the things he had to deal with all week, and expectations, the pressure, and you know, questioning whether or not he should be picked on the team or not. There's a lot of different things that were going on.

"And the way he came out and played this week and represented all of Canada was impressive."

American veteran Scott Verplank became just the

Fourth Day Singles Matches	
International	United States
7 Points	**5 Points**
Final Total	
International	United States
14½ Points	**19½ Points**

Former President George H.W. Bush was on the first tee to see off all the matches including Phil Mickelson and Vijay Singh.

seventh player to go unbeaten at The Presidents Cup, and the first since Stewart Cink and Davis Love III accomplished the feat in 2000. He partnered rookie Lucas Glover to two wins in Foursomes and picked up another with Steve Stricker in Four-ball before dispatching Rory Sabbatini 2 and 1 on Sunday.

And for the gritty man from Dallas, the chance to play for Nicklaus — Verplank still has the Golden Bear's autograph he got when he was eight — made the 2007 Presidents Cup even more special.

"You know, I just love playing team golf," Verplank said. "I have a pretty good record in the Ryder Cup, and I have a pretty good record in this just because I enjoy it so much. I feel like I'm a pretty good teammate and I know how to pick good teammates, too. This is a great event. ... Hope I get to play a few more."

Cink made his mark on Sunday, too, providing the winning U.S. point when he beat Nick O'Hern 6 and 4 in the most lopsided match of the week. The win was his third in four matches for the former Georgia Tech All-American, who set the tone for the day by starting off with five straight birdies.

"I was proud to be the one that did it, but credit doesn't go to me, it goes to everybody who teed the ball up this week, and everybody who did such a great job of staying in the game," Cink said. "I was so proud of everybody on this team and proud of myself, too. To win the final point, it was something that I didn't know happened at the time, but looking back, I'm proud of it."

The last time the U.S. had won an international team competition away from home was the 1993 Ryder Cup. These Americans, led by David Toms's 4½ points, had come into The Presidents Cup playing extremely well, though — winning six times and posting 17 top-10 finishes in their five starts prior to arriving at Royal Montreal.

The three U.S. rookies — Zach Johnson was a Presidents Cup newbie but already had a Ryder Cup under his belt — produced an additional 7½ points. Glover and Hunter Mahan, Nicklaus's two Captain's Picks, each won two matches, while Woody Austin went 1-1-3 and provided the Americans' emotional compass, not to mention the anchor of its highlight reel when he did that nosedive into the lake on Friday.

"It's just been the greatest week," said Austin, who spoofed himself by donning a diving mask on Sunday. "I talked to the other two rookies, Hunter and Lucas, about what we expected this week, and we all expected a fun week, but I could not have imagined this much fun. These guys, we all get to hang out a little bit on the TOUR, but it's more just you play your rounds. You see everyone every once in a while or whatever, but I don't get the opportunity to have dinner with Phil and Tiger and hang around them in their atmosphere or whatever.

"I've gotten a different perspective. I already know how great they are as players and how good they are as people when I'm with them on the golf course. But now I've got to know just how great they are even off the golf course ... they have been the funniest, greatest teammates I could ever have imagined.

"So if all comes to a close for me at this juncture, I couldn't have asked for a better week. If it continues, I'm going to bust my butt to get into another one, because it's been a blast and a half."

—*Helen Ross*

Stewart Cink provided the winning point of the match.

INDIVIDUAL POINTS TOTALS

 International

	Played	Won	Lost	Halved	Points
Mike Weir	5	3	1	1	3½
Ernie Els	5	3	2	0	3
Retief Goosen	5	2	2	1	2½
Vijay Singh	5	2	2	1	2½
Angel Cabrera	4	2	2	0	2
Stuart Appleby	5	2	3	0	2
Geoff Ogilvy	5	2	3	0	2
Adam Scott	5	1	3	1	1½
K.J. Choi	4	1	3	0	1
Nick O'Hern	5	1	4	0	1
Trevor Immelman	4	0	3	1	½
Rory Sabbatini	4	0	3	1	½

United States

	Played	Won	Lost	Halved	Points
David Toms	5	4	0	1	4½
Scott Verplank	4	4	0	0	4
Stewart Cink	4	3	1	0	3
Jim Furyk	5	3	2	0	3
Steve Stricker	5	3	2	0	3
Tiger Woods	5	3	2	0	3
Phil Mickelson	5	2	1	2	3
Woody Austin	5	1	1	3	2½
Charles Howell III	4	2	2	0	2
Zach Johnson	4	2	2	0	2
Lucas Glover	5	2	3	0	2
Hunter Mahan	5	2	3	0	2

Fourth Day Singles Match 23

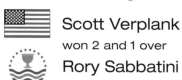

Scott Verplank
won 2 and 1 over
Rory Sabbatini

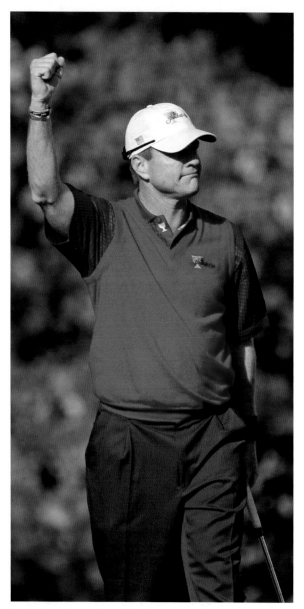

Scott Verplank came from 2 down to win on the 17th hole.

A mid-round swing adjustment, a lucky coin and a couple of late birdies were the difference in a taut duel that swung back and forth between two players who were among the most consistent all year on the PGA TOUR.

America's Scott Verplank, who won the Canadian Open at Royal Montreal in 2001, birdied three of the last six holes and recovered from a 2-down deficit to defeat South Africa's Rory Sabbatini, 2 and 1, in the day's opening Singles match. Verplank, who ran his record to 4-0 for the week and 3-0 in Singles in The Presidents Cup, suffered three bogeys on the first nine before pulling his game together and keeping Sabbatini winless for the week.

"I was getting quick from the top and being too steep," Verplank, 43, said after improving to 10-3-1 in combined team match play competition. "So I just slowed it down and became more shallow and hit the ball from the inside a bit more, and the stroke got better."

So did his chances against Sabbatini, who had his own struggles that he never deciphered, manifested in his finding just three fairways in 17 holes.

Charged with blunting a potential International rally, Verplank got off to a rousing start with a 30-footer for birdie at the par-4 opening hole, but Sabbatini's short birdie at the second squared the match. By the turn, Verplank was two behind with a trio of three-putt bogeys at the fourth, fifth and ninth holes that were mitigated only by Sabbatini's missed chances, including his own bogey at the third.

Sabbatini, who ranked second on the PGA TOUR in scrambling coming into the week, bogeyed the 10th

Verplank (left) won a coin toss to putt first on No. 16 and rolled home a 30-foot birdie that Rory Sabbatini could not match.

hole after a poor drive. That hiccup combined with a throat-clearing four-foot birdie putt by Verplank at the par-5 12th evened the score again.

The match eventually hinged on proceedings at the 456-yard par-4 16th hole. Both men faced birdie putts of around 30 feet. Verplank asked for a measurement, and it was simply too close to call, so a coin toss was used to determine the order of play. Verplank won the toss and promptly rammed in the putt. A stunned Sabbatini couldn't respond in kind.

On the following green, the par-3 17th, when Sabbatini missed a birdie putt from 14 feet and Ver-

plank converted from seven feet for birdie, the match was suddenly over, and Verplank had become just the seventh player in The Presidents Cup to post an unblemished record (no ties or losses).

"You know, I just love playing team golf," he said. "I have a pretty good record in the Ryder Cup, and I have a pretty good record in this event just because I enjoy it so much. I feel like I'm a pretty good teammate, and I know how to pick good teammates, too. This is a great event. Hope I get to play a few more."

—*Dave Shedloski*

Fourth Day Singles Match 23

Hole	1	2	3	4	5	6	7	8	9	10	11	12	13	14	15	16	17	18
Par	4	4	4	4	3	5	3	4	4	4	4	5	3	4	4	4	3	4
Status	1 up	AS	1 up	AS	-	-	-	-	-	-	-	AS	AS	AS	AS	1 up	2 up	
Scott Verplank	3C	4	4	5	4	5	3	4	5	4	4	4	3	4	4	3	2	
Rory Sabbatini	-	3	5	4	3	5	3	4	4	5	4	5	3	4	4	4	3	
Status	-	AS	-	AS	1 up	1 up	1 up	1 up	2 up	1 up	1 up	AS	AS	AS	AS	-	-	

Scott Verplank (U.S.) defeated Rory Sabbatini (International), 2 and 1.

Fourth Day Singles Match 24

Ernie Els

won 2 up over

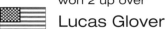

Lucas Glover

Lucas Glover was 3 up after six holes.

With a well-earned distinction as one of the most accomplished competitors in match play, Ernie Els wasn't about to take lightly a seemingly unthreatening encounter with rookie Lucas Glover in the day's second Singles match. He knew only too well that over 18 holes the line between favorite and underdog could be blurred easily.

Winner of seven HSBC World Match Play Championships, the Big Easy expected a hard-fought contest.

He got one.

Glover, who had made 12 birdies and an eagle in the first three days of the competition, birdied three of the first six holes to build a stunning 3-up lead before Els countered with his own blitz fueled by eight one-putt greens in the last 12 holes to eventually wear down the American. The result was a badly needed 2-up victory for the Internationals that briefly gave them some hope of a comeback.

Early on it looked like another American whitewash. While Els bogeyed two of the first six holes, Glover posted three birdies to lead 3 up — two of them set up by approaches inside five feet.

Fourth Day Singles Match 24																		
Hole	1	2	3	4	5	6	7	8	9	10	11	12	13	14	15	16	17	18
Par	4	4	4	4	3	5	3	4	4	4	4	5	3	4	4	4	3	4
Status	AS	AS	1 up	2 up	2 up	3 up	2 up	1 up	1 up	1 up	1 up	1 up	AS	-	AS	-	-	-
Lucas Glover	4	3	3	4	3	4	3	4	4	4	4	4	3	4	3	5	3	-
Ernie Els	4	3	4	5	3	6	2	3	4	4	4	4	2	3	4	4	3	C
Status	AS	AS	-	-	-	-	-	-	-	-	-	-	AS	1 up	AS	1 up	1 up	2 up

Ernie Els (International) defeated Lucas Glover (U.S.), 2 up.

Ernie Els came out of a bunker at No. 14 …

"I was in deep trouble the front nine," said Els, 37, who had not won a Singles match since 1998 when he edged Davis Love III. "I knew it was going to be tough. He made a ton of birdies, and I got off to a bit of a slow start, and somehow I battled my way back into the game."

The Big Easy's turnaround was remarkable. He birdied the seventh and eighth after a sloppy bogey at No. 6 and made the turn just 1 down. It took two more birdies to square the match as both men birdied the par-5 12th and then Els hit a laser into the 13th that stopped within three feet.

"I hit some beautiful shots coming in," Els said. "I needed that."

A third straight birdie at the 14th from 12 feet allowed the South African to nose ahead, but the resilient young American countered at the 15th with a kick-in birdie after an approach from 190 yards.

Of all things, a three-putt from 45 feet cost Glover a bogey at the 16th as he fell one behind. The two halved the par-3 17th, leaving Glover with only a chance for a tie at 18. But he played the final hole poorly and ended up with his ball in his pocket and "X" on the scorecard while conceding Els's birdie chance for the final margin.

… then holed the 11-foot putt to take the lead.

Els improved to 3-2 in Singles play, but in the immediate aftermath he wasn't thinking about personal records but of the Internationals getting back in the hunt.

"We needed to get off to a good start. Rory in front of me, I was watching him. He looked like he had it, not in the bag, but he was in control, and Scott made a beautiful putt on 16 and 17. But yeah, we need to get everything out of this match, we need a miracle in the bag and hopefully it can still happen."

—Dave Shedloski

Fourth Day Singles Match 25

Phil Mickelson
won 5 and 4 over
Vijay Singh

Hitting from the rough on the first hole, Phil Mickelson went on to a surprisingly easy win.

Vijay Singh was the only Singles player without a birdie.

An anticipated heavyweight battle between the only two men to compete in every Presidents Cup never materialized as Phil Mickelson, the No. 2 player in the world, dispatched No. 12 Vijay Singh with surprising ease to win his first Singles match in his seventh Presidents Cup start.

With the exception of the Tiger Woods-Mike Weir showdown, no match held more intrigue and potential for fireworks than this one. Mickelson and Singh had a well-publicized disagreement at the Masters over Mickelson's use of longer metal spikes, and Singh, when asked in a pre-tournament press conference about how he gets along with his left-handed rival, jokingly responded, "Phil Who?"

Members of the media had wondered if the match-up was pre-ordained, considering some of the perceived rancor between the two major champions, but U.S. Captain Jack Nicklaus dismissed that.

"It was Gary's pairing, he put Vijay out and I

thought it would be a good match. So I just put Phil with him," Nicklaus said.

It ended up as the second most lopsided decision of the final day. It also was the first match completed, taking just under three hours.

Singh was the only player among the 24 who failed to register a birdie on Sunday. His only lead was produced by Mickelson's nervous bogey at the opening hole.

Mickelson righted the ship quickly with his birdie-3 at the second, and he found himself ahead by two with simple pars when Singh bogeyed the third and sixth holes, the latter after he nearly hit his second shot out of bounds. In between, Singh converted miraculous par saves to stay in contention.

"I hit a terrible drive on the first hole, and ended up hitting it over the green and made bogey and gave him the hole. I believe that was the last fairway I missed," said Mickelson, who raised his overall Singles record in team competition (including the Ryder Cup) to 4-6-3. "I was able to play aggressive and attack pins and ended up making some birdies.

"He had a couple of great up-and-downs on Nos. 4 and 5, one of the best up-and-downs I'd ever seen. He was 50 yards left of the green on No. 4 in the trees and looked like he had no shot. He and I have played a lot of golf together in the last month or so, and I guess you play enough golf with someone, you start playing like him, because — (laughter) — he was hitting it like I usually do, and getting up-and-down."

After his bogey at No. 6, Singh had to concede

Mickelson watched the finish with wife Amy (left) and Sonia Toms.

a birdie at No. 7 and then fell four behind when Lefty birdied the 10th from seven feet. Mickelson two-putted for a birdie at the 12th while Singh three-putted from 60 feet to fall four behind. Singh, who fell to 1-4-2 in Singles, missed a nine-footer for the halve, and the die was cast.

Mickelson closed out the match with two routine pars.

"I knew that I needed to play well, and I'm fortunate that I got off to enough of a lead that we could wrap this up early," Mickelson said. "I didn't know what my record was, but it is nice to get a win. I was excited to have a chance to play against Vijay. It was a fun match, and I feel like I played well and had control for quite a long time."

—Dave Shedloski

Fourth Day Singles Match 25																		
Hole	1	2	3	4	5	6	7	8	9	10	11	12	13	14	15	16	17	18
Par	4	4	4	4	3	5	3	4	4	4	4	5	3	4	4	4	3	4
Status	-	AS	1 up	1 up	1 up	2 up	3 up	3 up	3 up	4 up	4 up	5 up	5 up	5 up				
Phil Mickelson	5	3	4	4	3	5	C	4	4	3	4	4	3	4				
Vijay Singh	4	4	5	4	3	6	-	4	4	4	4	5	3	4				
Status	1 up	AS	-	-	-	-	-	-	-	-	-	-	-	-				

Phil Mickelson (U.S.) defeated Vijay Singh (International), 5 and 4.

Fourth Day Singles Match 26

Mike Weir
won 1 up over
Tiger Woods

Tiger Woods hit from the rough on No. 18 after driving into the water.

This fourth match Sunday wasn't just about playing the best player in the world. Or staying focused in a crazy-loud wild atmosphere that only Tiger Woods — and maybe Phil Mickelson — can truly understand.

The match was about Mike Weir. About a man who had lobbied loud and hard to bring The Presidents Cup to his country; a man who had to answer questions about why he was a picked for the International Team in the first place.

When Woods failed to chip in at the 18th hole Sunday afternoon at Royal Montreal, he handed his club to caddie Stevie Williams and walked straight to Weir with an outstretched hand. The roar was deafening.

"I was glad I gave them something to cheer about at the end," Weir said of the 1-up win.

It was the moment of a lifetime.

"To play Tiger, he's the best there is," Weir said.

To beat him? With the country watching? International Captain Gary Player shook his head.

"Lord, can you imagine the pressure on him?" Player said of the final hole. "This could turn his life around."

In four days, Weir validated Player's selection of

Fourth Day Singles Match 26

Hole	1	2	3	4	5	6	7	8	9	10	11	12	13	14	15	16	17	18
Par	4	4	4	4	3	5	3	4	4	4	4	5	3	4	4	4	3	4
Status	AS	-	-	-	-	-	-	-	-	-	-	-	-	AS	1 up	1 up	AS	-
Tiger Woods	4	4	4	5	3	-	2	4	4	4	3	4	3	4	C	4	3	5
Mike Weir	4	3	4	4	3	C	2	4	4	4	4	5	3	5	-	4	2	3
Status	AS	1 up	1 up	2 up	2 up	3 up	3 up	3 up	3 up	3 up	2 up	1 up	1 up	AS	-	-	AS	1 up

Mike Weir (International) defeated Tiger Woods (U.S.), 1 up.

him as a Captain's Pick and that swing change. All he did was lead his team with a 3-1-1 record, shoulder the job as genial host, and beat the best player in the world. In a comeback.

"For the pressure that he had all week, it was pretty phenomenal how he had to deal with that and the way he played," Woods said. "And the way he came out and played this week and represented all of Canada was impressive."

Weir earned the right to face Tiger and took it straight to the No. 1 player in the world. He went 3 up after six holes and hung on until the ninth hole when he missed a six-footer for birdie. And the chance to go 4 up. Ditto for the 10th hole when he two-putted from nine feet.

Those two halves were the cracks Woods needed. He cut Weir's lead to 2 up when he hit to six inches at the 11th, then put the ball just less than three feet from the cup at the 12th to whittle Weir's lead to 1 up. Woods squared the match at the 14th when Weir missed a five-footer for par, and went 1 up when Weir hit his approach into the water at No. 15 and conceded that hole.

"I just kept telling myself I'm playing well," Weir said. "I kept telling myself to be patient. ... And once he got ahead, I wasn't going to let him finish it off early. I was going to fight until the end."

Weir went for it. He struck the ball to 10 feet at the 17th and one-putted, while Woods two-putted from 12 feet. The match was all-square going to No. 18.

Weir's drive found the fairway, Woods's found the water. But even then Tiger gave himself a chance, trying to chip in for par to force Weir to two-putt from 15 feet. When Tiger's chip came up six inches away, he conceded Weir's putt and the match.

"But I expected him to chip that in at the end there, and he almost did," Weir said. "That's just Tiger, and he's a class act."

—*Melanie Hauser*

Mike Weir holed from 10 feet at No. 17 to square the match.

Fourth Day Singles Match 27

Angel Cabrera

won 2 and 1 over

Woody Austin

Angel Cabrera had no bogeys in the Singles and only five bogeys for the week.

This was the battle of two of 2007's most unlikely stars. Angel Cabrera, the reigning U.S. Open champion, vs. Woody Austin, golf's newest legend.

Coming into the season they were your basic veteran players. The lumbering Argentinean with a streaky game. The former bank teller with a penchant for self-deprecation and a short temper with his putter.

Then Cabrera outlasted Tiger Woods at Oakmont for the 2007 U.S. Open title and Austin played his way onto the U.S. Team with a win at the Stanford St. Jude Classic and a runner-up finish to Woods at the PGA Championship. And, he provided the most memorable shot of the year when he flopped into the lake trying to hit a shot at the 14th hole Friday before shaking it off to birdie the next three holes.

"Obviously he expects a lot of himself and sometimes probably too much of himself," Jim Furyk said of Austin. "But you can never fault him for not trying, for not giving 100 percent. He obviously pokes fun at himself, so it's easy for everyone else to kind of climb on board."

Which they did even before the dive, when the only question his teammates had was how he was going to perform in a plain team Presidents Cup shirt instead of his signature bright patterns. The answer was quite well. And well enough Sunday to join Cabrera in a nail-biter.

Of course, it was also a little entertaining when Austin pulled out a diving mask at the 14th hole and got everyone laughing. But in the end, it was Cabrera's no-bogey round — the only one of the day — that made the difference.

The new-found folk hero scraped and scraped to keep up with Cabrera, who was hitting some incredible shots. Like at the second hole when Austin was eight feet from the cup and Cabrera carved out a shot from behind a tree and dropped it softly to two feet for a halve.

On the next hole, Austin got into trouble, bogeyed, and Cabrera, who had just five bogeys all week, two-putted for par and a 1-up lead. Austin squared the match at the sixth, went 1 down at the seventh and squared it again at the eighth.

Austin's three-putt bogey from 40 feet at the ninth gave Cabrera the lead for good, 1 up, and Cabrera dropped a 10-footer at the 10th hole to go 2 up. Austin kept it close, cutting the lead back to 1 up with a birdie at No. 11, but when he had the chance to square the match at No. 14, he left his 16-footer for birdie just short.

Cabrera, who hopes to see The Presidents Cup played in South America one day, closed it out at the 17th when Austin's 13-foot birdie putt didn't fall and

Woody Austin was a hit with his diving mask.

he drilled his seven-footer for the win and a consistent career Presidents Cup record of 3-3-3.

Austin finished the week 1-1-3 and couldn't wait for another chance in team competition.

"I've gotten a different perspective," Austin said. "I couldn't have asked for a better week. If it continues, I'm going to bust my butt to get into another one, because it's been a blast and a half."

—Melanie Hauser

Fourth Day Singles Match 27

Hole	1	2	3	4	5	6	7	8	9	10	11	12	13	14	15	16	17	18
Par	4	4	4	4	3	5	3	4	4	4	4	5	3	4	4	4	3	4
Status	AS	AS	-	-	-	AS	-	AS	-	-	-	-	-	-	-	-	-	
Woody Austin	4	3	5	4	3	4	3	3	5	4	3	4	3	4	4	3	3	
Angel Cabrera	4	3	4	4	3	5	2	4	4	3	4	4	3	4	3	4	2	
Status	AS	AS	1 up	1 up	1 up	AS	1 up	AS	1 up	2 up	1 up	1 up	1 up	1 up	2 up	1 up	2 up	

Angel Cabrera (International) defeated Woody Austin (U.S.), 2 and 1.

Fourth Day Singles Match 28

Adam Scott
won 2 and 1 over
Zach Johnson

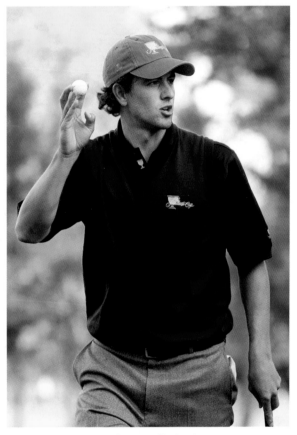

Seven birdies lifted Adam Scott to a Singles victory.

Talk about salvaging a bad week.

Adam Scott struggled for the first three days. A flash of brilliance here, a missed putt there. No full points. One halve. Not what you would expect from the No. 6 player in the world.

Not what Scott expected.

But overnight everything changed. Scott dialed in his irons, putts started to fall, and Zach Johnson, another of the world's best young players, wound up as collateral damage.

Scott won the first Singles match of his Presidents Cup career by a score of 2 and 1. He birdied seven of the first 17 holes and four of those birdies were from inside 10 feet, including the winning five-footer at the 17th. But it wasn't exactly a stroll around Royal Montreal.

Johnson, who finished the week 2-2, wasn't the least bit rattled. After Scott birdied the first hole from six feet, the 2007 Masters champion squared it with an 18-footer at the second, and the battle was on.

Scott, who won the Shell Houston Open earlier in the year, opened a 2-up lead, but Johnson won the 10th and 11th holes — the former with a 25-foot roller coaster — to square it again. Scott took the lead

Fourth Day Singles Match 28																		
Hole	1	2	3	4	5	6	7	8	9	10	11	12	13	14	15	16	17	18
Par	4	4	4	4	3	5	3	4	4	4	4	5	3	4	4	4	3	4
Status	-	AS	AS	AS	-	-	-	-	-	-	AS	-	-	-	-	-	-	
Zach Johnson	4	3	4	5	3	5	2	4	4	4	4	5	3	4	3	4	3	
Adam Scott	3	4	4	5	2	4	2	4	4	4	5	4	3	3	5	4	2	
Status	1 up	AS	AS	AS	1 up	2 up	2 up	2 up	2 up	1 up	AS	1 up	1 up	2 up	1 up	1 up	2 up	

Adam Scott (International) defeated Zach Johnson (U.S.), 2 and 1.

Zach Johnson never led but was only 1 down to Scott with two holes to play.

for good at the 12th with a six-footer for birdie. Then Scott missed the green at the 13th and chipped to two inches. Johnson birdied the 15th from 13 feet to cut the lead to 1 up, but Scott closed it out at the 17th.

"It's disappointing for us, but I felt I played better every day, and it's just hard-fought matches," Scott said. "The U.S. played great throughout the week and we left ourselves a lot to do today."

The match salvaged a so-so week for Scott, whose goal was to improve his Singles record, which was 0-2. He lost to Jim Furyk 3 and 2 in 2005 and to Charles Howell III 5 and 4 in 2003.

"Our Singles are so important," Scott said before the matches began. "My record is dismal and that's something I'd like to change this week for sure.

"Singles matches are tough and it's a grind. No matter who you play, it's 18 holes of match play, and it's a little unpredictable. So I think me personally, from my experience, I need to knuckle down a little bit more and every shot counts twice as much."

He entered the week 3-0-1 in Foursomes, but struggled. He and Geoff Ogilvy lost the first match of The Presidents Cup to Steve Stricker and Hunter Mahan 3 and 2, then he and K.J. Choi lost a Four-ball match to Stricker and Scott Verplank 2 and 1. The toughest match was Saturday morning when he and Ernie Els ran into a wall against Tiger Woods and Jim Furyk, who cruised to a 4-and-3 win.

Scott sat out the afternoon Four-ball Saturday. Perhaps the rest was all he needed.

—*Melanie Hauser*

Fourth Day Singles Match 29

David Toms
won 2 up over

Trevor Immelman

David Toms was near-perfect with 4½ points.

An award for best supporting player at Royal Montreal could have gone to David Toms. Four different partners in four matches. A 2-up Singles win over Trevor Immelman.

And the most points by any player in the field — 4½.

Toms, the 2001 PGA Championship winner and perennial U.S. Team member, was really never in the spotlight. Unless, of course, you count the shots of him laughing when Woody Austin took his tumble into the water Friday.

The master of quiet understatement came into The Presidents Cup in less than top form. A strong early 2007 had given way to a so-so two months that included a pair of missed cuts and a withdrawal. Then there was the matter of his career record in this competition — 2-7.

The quiet Louisiana native turned it around at Royal Montreal. He paired with Jim Furyk for an opening Foursomes win over Ernie Els and Angel Cabrera, then followed it up playing straight man to Woody Austin's Aqua Man in a Four-ball halve with Trevor Immelman and Rory Sabbatini. Saturday, Toms and Zach Johnson dispatched Nick O'Hern and Geoff Ogilvy 2 and 1, then he and Woods took down O'Hern and Ogilvy 5 and 3 in Four-ball.

"I got some good partners this week," he said. "I played with Tiger when he was playing well, and Woody Austin, the way he finished up one day, and today I played well. Overall I think it's attributed to the fact that I played pretty solid, and I was stuck with some good partners."

He also had enough left to beat Immelman in Singles.

Toms's opening 11 holes against the South African were shaky. He missed five putts inside 21 feet, but still led 1 up. Immelman had taken the first lead of the match with a birdie at the sixth hole, but Toms took the lead on a pair of pars at the eighth and ninth.

Two putts from 50 feet at the par-5 12th gave Toms his first birdie of the match and a 2-up lead, and he went 3 up at the 14th after nearly driving the green at the 369-yard par-4. Ironically, it was the same hole where both he and Austin dunked their tee shots Friday.

Birdies on the 15th and 16th holes brought Trevor Immelman within one, but he drove into the water at the last.

Immelman rallied with back-to-back birdies at the 15th and 16th holes to send the match to the 18th. Immelman shattered any hopes of a halve when his tee shot on No. 18 went left and into the water.

With a par to Immelman's bogey, Toms won the match 2 up.

When asked what he would remember most about the week, Toms said: "I think our team. We really had a good mix of young guys and some old guys like myself and we just seemed to gel really well together, and we practiced really well and we just had fun. That's what usually happens; when you have fun, you play good golf, and we did that this week."

Toms's 4½ points was second-most in Presidents Cup history behind Mark O'Meara (1996) and Shigeki Maruyama (1998), who each had a perfect 5 points.

—*Melanie Hauser*

Fourth Day Singles Match 29

Hole	1	2	3	4	5	6	7	8	9	10	11	12	13	14	15	16	17	18
Par	4	4	4	4	3	5	3	4	4	4	4	5	3	4	4	4	3	4
Status	AS	AS	AS	AS	AS	-	-	AS	1 up	1 up	1 up	2 up	2 up	3 up	2 up	1 up	1 up	2 up
David Toms	5	4	4	4	3	5	3	4	4	4	4	4	3	3	4	4	3	4
Trevor Immelman	5	4	4	4	3	4	3	5	5	4	4	5	3	4	3	3	3	5
Status	AS	AS	AS	AS	AS	1 up	1 up	AS	-	-	-	-	-	-	-	-	-	-

David Toms (U.S.) defeated Trevor Immelman (International), 2 up.

Fourth Day Singles Match 30

Stewart Cink
won 6 and 4 over
Nick O'Hern

Stewart Cink hit to the 14th green, his last full shot.

It started out as just another match near the middle of the lineup. A solid American team staple against an International player best known for taking down Tiger Woods. Twice.

It wound up being the rout that clinched The Presidents Cup.

Nick O'Hern never had a chance. Stewart Cink, your ultimate team player, morphed into a buzz saw in his final two matches. The man who missed a big putt Friday afternoon birdied four of his last seven holes in Saturday's Four-ball win with Jim Furyk and really turned it on Sunday in his 6-and-4 defeat of O'Hern.

Can you say birdies on the first five holes and six of the first nine? He was 5 up after eight holes and 4 up at the turn after losing the ninth with a par. Whew.

And in case you're wondering, that first stretch of putts were, in order, from 39 feet, 2 feet, 11 feet, 33 feet and 3½ feet.

"We came into this week with a little score to settle up in the international golf arena, and I think we showed everybody that we can play again," Cink said.

Fourth Day Singles Match 30																		
Hole	1	2	3	4	5	6	7	8	9	10	11	12	13	14	15	16	17	18
Par	4	4	4	4	3	5	3	4	4	4	4	5	3	4	4	4	3	4
Status	AS	1 up	2 up	3 up	4 up	3 up	4 up	5 up	4 up	3 up	3 up	4 up	5 up	6 up				
Stewart Cink	3	3	3	3	2	5	3	3	4	4	5	4	3	C				
Nick O'Hern	3	4	4	4	3	4	4	4	3	3	5	5	4	-				
Status	AS	-	-	-	-	-	-	-	-	-	-	-	-	-				

Stewart Cink (U.S.) defeated Nick O'Hern (International), 6 and 4.

Cink certainly did. He erased any doubts stemming from the 3½-foot putt he missed at the 17th hole Friday — the one that cost him and Lucas Glover a halve in their match with O'Hern and Geoff Ogilvy — when he went 10-under par during that 19-hole stretch over two days. He did it with radar irons and smooth putts. And a confidence that stood up to, then squashed, O'Hern's gritty comeback.

Yes, O'Hern birdied the ninth and 10th holes to trim the deficit to 3 down, but after both bogeyed the 11th, Cink won the next three holes — two with birdies — to close out the match. It was the widest margin since 2000 when Carlos Franco beat Hal Sutton 6 and 5.

It was a quiet celebration at the 14th. With his teammates scattered all around the course, he had caddie Frank Williams and wife Lisa to congratulate him on the win and on his 3-1 record for the week.

"When you're by yourself and you've won, that means you won your match early and I'm happy to do that," Cink said. "In match play you don't want to keep playing golf when you're ahead. I'm happy to be the one to clinch the point for the U.S. Team."

O'Hern, who has beaten Woods twice in the World Golf Championships–Accenture Match Play Championship, ended the matches with a dismal 1-4 record.

"I think our pairings were very good," O'Hern said. "You know, we just — that 18th hole didn't treat us very kindly.

"As Geoff (Ogilvy) said, maybe we didn't play to our full potential, but we played some good golf. You've got to hand it to the U.S., they played very well. It's a tough format. If you take the Foursomes out of it, if we lose the Foursomes 3-2 or 4-2, we almost won The Presidents Cup.

"I think there should be four matches of Four-ball next time."

—*Melanie Hauser*

Cink was greeted by Jack Nicklaus.

Nick O'Hern never had a chance against the hot Cink.

Fourth Day Singles Match 31

Geoff Ogilvy
won 1 up over
Steve Stricker

Geoff Ogilvy was ahead for most of the match, but had to win No. 18 for the victory.

In a match between past winners of the World Golf Championships–Accenture Match Play Championship, Geoff Ogilvy and Steve Stricker pushed each other to the limit before Stricker, so solid all week, faltered on the last hole to let the Australian escape 1 up.

"There's no science behind it. You've just got to play better," Ogilvy said in trying to explain how he and his International teammates fell so far behind over the first three days of The Presidents Cup.

Ogilvy took some of his own advice to heart, playing fairly steady at the start and putting on a late

kick at the end. He began with a two-putt birdie at the par-4 second hole, which set him up for a 1-up lead. Stricker answered with his own birdie on the sixth, but a short putt for birdie at the eighth allowed Ogilvy to nose ahead again.

A routine par at the 10th doubled the advantage when Stricker couldn't save par after missing the green.

Stricker needed a break, and Ogilvy inexplicably provided it when he bogeyed the par-5 12th, the only player to score higher than par on the hole on the final day. Rejuvenated, the American jumped on his

Steve Stricker conceded on the 18th green.

Gary Player and Ogilvy looked on.

next opportunity, holing an 18-footer for birdie at the par-3 13th to bring the match back to even.

Stricker wasn't done. He forged ahead when he reached the par-4 14th hole in two shots. Ogilvy conceded the short second putt for birdie.

That was the Australian's wake-up call. He saved par and a halve at No. 15, and then sank a 26-foot birdie at the 16th to knot up the proceedings one last time. Both players had a good look at birdie at the next, but Ogilvy misfired from 25 feet and Stricker from 21 feet, sending the match to the final hole.

On the tough par-4 18th, the normally accurate Stricker picked a bad time to get wild. His drive drifted into the rough and his second shot was sliced so far to the right that it cleared the grandstand as well as a row of hedges toward the practice green. It took more than 10 minutes to find relief from the grandstands and play his next shot, which went through the green.

With Ogilvy safely on in two and within range of the cup, Stricker conceded the birdie, and with it the match. He was disappointed in the finish, but not the proceedings on the whole.

"Three years ago I was fighting for my card and now to be a part of this is remarkable and unbelievable at times. So, just fortunate — fortunate to be a part of this," Stricker said. "We had a great week. What can I say? I'm at a loss for words. But I had so much fun with the guys and got to reconnect with a lot of them that I had not seen for so many years because of my poor play. This week it's all about the team."

—Dave Shedloski

Fourth Day Singles Match 31

Hole	1	2	3	4	5	6	7	8	9	10	11	12	13	14	15	16	17	18
Par	4	4	4	4	3	5	3	4	4	4	4	5	3	4	4	4	3	4
Status	AS	-	-	-	-	AS	AS	-	-	-	-	-	AS	1 up	1 up	AS	AS	-
Steve Stricker	4	4	4	4	3	4	3	4	4	5	4	5	2	C	4	4	3	-
Geoff Ogilvy	4	3	4	4	3	5	3	3	4	4	4	6	3	-	4	3	3	C
Status	AS	1 up	1 up	1 up	1 up	AS	AS	1 up	1 up	2 up	2 up	1 up	AS	-	-	AS	AS	1 up

Geoff Ogilvy (International) defeated Steve Stricker (U.S.), 1 up.

Fourth Day Singles Match 32

K.J. Choi
won 3 and 2 over

Hunter Mahan

K.J. Choi scored his first point on the last day.

Hunter Mahan said he 'ran out of gas.'

K.J. Choi, a two-time PGA TOUR winner in 2007 and one of a handful of contenders for the FedExCup title up until the last tournament, was the only player for either side without so much as a half-point heading into the final day.

The talented South Korean, who a month prior to The Presidents Cup had to withdraw from the Deutsche Bank Championship because of a nagging back injury, undoubtedly was feeling some pressure after a series of setbacks. He responded by transferring that pressure onto young Hunter Mahan after a shaky start, and eventually he ran off to a face-saving 3-and-2 victory in the third-to-last match.

"Yes, I was in some very strong matches," said Choi, who improved to 2-0 in Singles matches. "The last three days, I couldn't make the putts, and it was a little tough. ... It was good to have a win in the Singles."

Mahan, who played splendidly in the team sessions in his first Presidents Cup, was more charitable to his opponent going solo, shooting two over par over 16 holes and converting just two birdies. He didn't wait long to give Choi some hope when he double-bogeyed the second hole after taking four to get down

Fourth Day Singles Match 32																		
Hole	1	2	3	4	5	6	7	8	9	10	11	12	13	14	15	16	17	18
Par	4	4	4	4	3	5	3	4	4	4	4	5	3	4	4	4	3	4
Status	AS	-	-	AS	1 up	AS	AS	AS	1 up	AS	AS	AS	AS	-	-	-		
Hunter Mahan	4	6	4	4	3	5	3	4	3	4	4	4	3	4	5	5		
K.J. Choi	4	4	4	5	4	4	3	4	4	3	4	4	3	3	4	4		
Status	AS	1 up	1 up	AS	-	AS	AS	AS	-	AS	AS	AS	AS	1 up	2 up	3 up		

K.J. Choi (International) defeated Hunter Mahan (U.S.), 3 and 2.

Arm-in-arm with K.J. Choi, Jack Nicklaus shook hands with Hunter Mahan.

from the edge of the green.

Choi, who came into The Presidents Cup among the top 10 on the PGA TOUR in scoring, scrambling and sand saves, was equally amiable in the early going. His three-putt bogeys at the fourth and fifth holes reversed the scoreboard to leave him a hole behind, but the man nicknamed "Tank" got back on track and made par or better the rest of the match, starting with his two-foot birdie at the par-5 sixth that squared the tally.

After matching pars on the next two holes, Mahan made the turn at 1 up by winning the ninth with the first of his two birdies from about 12 feet.

The match stayed even from Nos. 10 through 13, with both players scoring birdies at the 12th.

Choi finally halted the impasse when he knocked in a six-footer for birdie on No. 14 after hitting into a bunker.

Feeling pressed, Mahan found the water at the par-4 15th to card a bogey, and Choi's routine par at the tough 16th was good enough to end the match when Mahan found a greenside bunker and then failed to convert his 17-foot par attempt.

"I kind of ran out of gas," Mahan admitted. "But I can't say I'm disappointed with the way the week turned out."

Despite his struggles, Choi had no complaints either. "Yes, I had very good time," he said.

—*Dave Shedloski*

Fourth Day Singles Match 33

Charles Howell III

won 2 and 1 over

Stuart Appleby

Charles Howell III had five consecutive birdies.

Stuart Appleby lost in Singles for the fifth time. .

In 2005, Stuart Appleby was Chris DiMarco's foil in Singles, watching helplessly as the American drained a 15-footer on the 18th hole of the final match of the day to give the United States the hard-earned victory.

At Royal Montreal two years later, the Australian found himself in the penultimate pairing on Sunday. The outcome was the same, though, as Charles Howell III handled Appleby his fifth Singles defeat in as many Presidents Cups and the U.S. won again.

From the outset, Appleby was wary of Howell, who had a win and two runner-up finishes in his first five events of 2007, before cooling off down the stretch. "I hope Charles doesn't play anything like he did at the start of the year, or I'll be in for a real, real tough match, more tough than I want," the Aussie had said Saturday evening.

Turns out, Appleby's worst fears were realized.

The first nine was very close, with Howell leading 1 up three times before sending the match back to all square when he three-putted No. 9 for bogey. The American then drove into the water on the 10th hole and suddenly found himself trailing Appleby for the first time Sunday.

Howell shook off that miscue, though, and seized control with a string of five straight birdies starting at the 11th hole — rolling in putts of 15, 6, 20, 9 and 14 feet. The first three gave Howell a 2-up advantage, the fourth got him a halve, and the fifth put the American dormie at 3 up.

Howell's bogey at the 16th hole gave Appleby a glimmer of hope, but the American picked up the 2-and-1 victory when he matched the Aussie's birdie at No. 17 with a 17-footer of his own. The victory gave

Howell rolled in a 17-foot putt on No. 17 to win the match.

Howell a 2-2-0 record this year, while Appleby, who struggled off the tee, missing four of his first five fairways and two of his last three, went 2-3-0.

"It was tough," said Howell, who was playing in his second Presidents Cup. "My last seven holes, I had six birdies, so it was a tough match and Stuart played well. Just I had the putter working a little bit better at the end."

Howell had to be happy with his overall record, which included a Foursomes win in tandem with his good friend Tiger Woods. The common goal, and the commonality of his teammates, would be his most vivid memories, though.

"It's amazing how much pressure you feel on the course just because you're playing for a team and for a country," Howell said. "But the memories off the golf course, you just get to know these guys a whole lot better and they have all got a lot in common."

—*Helen Ross*

Fourth Day Singles Match 33																		
Hole	1	2	3	4	5	6	7	8	9	10	11	12	13	14	15	16	17	18
Par	4	4	4	4	3	5	3	4	4	4	4	5	3	4	4	4	3	4
Status	AS	1 up	1 up	AS	1 up	1 up	AS	1 up	AS	-	AS	1 up	2 up	2 up	3 up	2 up	2 up	
Charles Howell III	4	3	4	5	3	5	3	3	5	-	3	4	2	3	3	5	2	
Stuart Appleby	4	4	4	4	4	5	2	4	4	C	4	5	3	3	5	4	2	
Status	AS	-	-	AS	-	-	AS	-	AS	1 up	AS	-	-	-	-	-	-	

Charles Howell III (U.S.) defeated Stuart Appleby (International), 2 and 1.

Fourth Day Singles Match 34

Retief Goosen
won 2 and 1 over
Jim Furyk

Retief Goosen won 2½ points for the week.

Jim Furyk lost for the first time in Singles.

Retief Goosen, who had been the Man of the Match for the Internationals in 2005 in a losing effort, was surprisingly quiet in this renewal.

As he entered his Singles match with Jim Furyk, who was the No. 3-ranked player in the world, Goosen had won just one match at Royal Montreal, teaming with Angel Cabrera to beat Phil Mickelson and Hunter Mahan in Four-ball. His record overall was 1-2-1, indicative of the International Team's struggles overall.

Furyk had never been beaten in four previous Singles matches at The Presidents Cup, while Goosen's 2-1 record was none-too-shabby, either — and included a 2-and-1 victory over Woods in 2005. With the United States leading by seven points entering Sunday's competition, though, this match, in the day's finale, wasn't expected to figure prominently in the outcome.

Furyk took the early 2-up lead when he holed a shot from the fairway for an eagle at the second hole and Goosen made bogey at No. 4. The South African must have been chapped by his miscue, though, because Goosen came back with a vengeance — winning four of the next five holes with birdies, including three straight putts from inside 10 feet starting at No. 7, to move to 2 up.

Goosen gave one hole back with a bogey at No. 13, but won the next when Furyk hooked his drive into the lake that had claimed so many victims during the week — and provided The Presidents Cup's signature moment as Woody Austin tumbled into the water. Furyk narrowed the gap to 1 down when he won the 16th hole as Goosen made a water-logged bogey of his own.

The South African was undaunted, though, as he

coolly rolled in a 10-footer on No. 17 to earn the final International point.

"It's been an exciting week but we lost in the Foursomes, so better luck next time," the taciturn Goosen said. "It went okay this week (for him personally). I putted terrible this week, but today I hit the ball nicely and made a few putts. Jim Furyk was 2 up very quickly on me and suddenly I started making a few birdies."

Furyk, for his part, didn't mull over what might have been. He was too busy enjoying the American victory, its fifth in seven Presidents Cups.

"You all see it, I'm sure you all feel it; I see it and I feel it, that we're a little bit more loose this week. I think we have a little bit more fun and enjoy it this week," he said. "Why that translates over into our play, I'm not sure. I go to the Ryder Cups thinking that I'm going to loosen up and I'm going to enjoy the week and I'm always a little bit tighter. I have fun, but I'm always a little tighter there than I am at a Presidents Cup.

"I've got no answer. The team we beat is one hell of a team, from top to bottom, 12 guys that are all very, very solid players. You all said that they look better on paper than we do, and that's true.

"But I'll tell you, it seems like we pull together, we have a hell of a time, and we're loose for these weeks at The Presidents Cup and we tend to gel more. I have no answer for you why that would be, but it sure is fun to ride it while we're here."

—*Helen Ross*

Goosen said he 'hit the ball nicely.'

Fourth Day Singles Match 34

Hole	1	2	3	4	5	6	7	8	9	10	11	12	13	14	15	16	17	18
Par	4	4	4	4	3	5	3	4	4	4	4	5	3	4	4	4	3	4
Status	AS	1 up	1 up	2 up	1 up	1 up	AS	-	-	-	-	-	-	-	-	-	-	
Jim Furyk	4	2	4	4	3	5	3	5	4	4	4	5	3	5	4	3	3	
Retief Goosen	4	3	4	5	2	5	2	3	3	4	4	5	4	3	4	5	2	
Status	AS	-	-	-	-	-	AS	1 up	2 up	2 up	2 up	2 up	1 up	2 up	2 up	1 up	2 up	

Retief Goosen (International) defeated Jim Furyk (U.S.), 2 and 1.

Records

Widest margin of victory

11 points   United States def. International, 2000, $21^1/_2$-$10^1/_2$

9 points   International def. United States, 1998, $20^1/_2$-$11^1/_2$

Smallest margin of victory

1 point   United States def. International, 1996, $16^1/_2$-$15^1/_2$

Most matches played

35   Vijay Singh, International (1994, 1996, 1998, 2000, 2003, 2005, 2007)

33   Phil Mickelson, U.S. (1994, 1996, 1998, 2000, 2003, 2005, 2007)

Most matches won

16   Davis Love III, U.S. (16-8-4)

14   Vijay Singh, International (14-15-6)

13   Ernie Els, International (13-10-2)

      Jim Furyk, U.S. (13-8-2)

      Tiger Woods, U.S. (13-11-1)

Most matches lost

15   Vijay Singh, International (14-15-6)

14   Stuart Appleby, International (5-14-2)

13   Phil Mickelson, U.S. (11-13-9)

Most matches halved

9   Phil Mickelson, U.S. (11-13-9)

6   Vijay Singh, International (14-15-6)

4   Nick Price, International (8-11-4)

Most matches won in one year

5   Mark O'Meara, U.S. (1996)

     Shigeki Maruyama, International (1998)

Most matches lost in one year

5   Ernie Els, International (2000)

     Phil Mickelson, U.S. (2003)

Most matches halved in one year

3   Angel Cabrera, International (2005)

Shortest match

12 holes   David Frost (International) def. Kenny Perry (U.S.), 7 and 6 (1996)

13 holes   11 times

Played with same partner most times

6   Ernie Els/Vijay Singh, International

5   Phil Mickelson/Tom Lehman, U.S.

     Phil Mickelson/Chris DiMarco, U.S.

Most Four-ball matches played

14   Vijay Singh, International (8-5-1)

12   Davis Love III, U.S. (7-4-1)

Most Four-ball matches won

8   Vijay Singh, International (8-5-1)

Most Four-ball matches lost

7   Tiger Woods, U.S. (3-7-0)

5   Frank Nobilo, International (0-5-0)

     Nick Price, International (3-5-2)

     Vijay Singh, International (8-5-1)

Most Foursomes matches played

14	Vijay Singh, International (6-6-2)
13	Phil Mickelson, U.S. (5-6-2)
10	Davis Love III, U.S. (5-3-2)
	Ernie Els, International (4-5-1)
	Tiger Woods, U.S. (7-2-1)

Most Foursomes matches won

7	Tiger Woods, U.S. (7-2-1)

Most Foursomes matches lost

6	Phil Mickelson, U.S. (5-6-2)
	Vijay Singh, International (5-6-3)
	Stuart Appleby, International (1-6-2)

Most Singles matches played

7	Phil Mickelson, U.S. (1-3-3)
	Vijay Singh, International (1-4-2)
6	Davis Love III, U.S. (4-1-1)

Most Singles matches won

4	Jim Furyk, U.S. (4-1-0)
	Davis Love III, U.S. (4-1-1)
3	Tiger Woods, U.S. (3-2-0)
	Craig Parry, International (3-0-0)
	Fred Couples, U.S. (3-0-1)
	Ernie Els, International (3-2-0)
	Retief Goosen, International (3-1-0)
	Mike Weir, International (3-1-0)

Most Singles matches lost

5	Stuart Appleby, International (0-5-0)
4	Nick Price, International (1-4-0)
	Vijay Singh, International (1-4-2)
3	Justin Leonard, U.S. (1-3-0)
	Phil Mickelson, U.S. (1-3-3)
	Adam Scott, International (0-3-0)

Results/Future Sites

Year	Venue	Score (Captains)
1994	Robert Trent Jones Golf Club Prince William County, Virginia	United States 20, International 12 (Hale Irwin) (David Graham)
1996	Robert Trent Jones Golf Club Prince William County, Virginia	United States 16½, International 15½ (Arnold Palmer) (Peter Thomson)
1998	Royal Melbourne Golf Club Melbourne, Australia	International 20½, United States 11½ (Peter Thomson) (Jack Nicklaus)
2000	Robert Trent Jones Golf Club Prince William County, Virginia	United States 21½, International 10½ (Ken Venturi) (Peter Thomson)
2003	The Links at Fancourt George, South Africa	International 17, United States 17 (Gary Player) (Jack Nicklaus)
2005	Robert Trent Jones Golf Club Prince William County, Virginia	United States 18½, International 15½ (Jack Nicklaus) (Gary Player)
2007	The Royal Montreal Golf Club Montreal, Quebec, Canada	United States 19½, International 14½ (Jack Nicklaus) (Gary Player)
		Total: United States 5, International 1, Tie 1
2009	Harding Park Golf Course San Francisco, California	
2011	Royal Melbourne Golf Club Melbourne, Australia	

THE PRESIDENTS CUP 2007

ISBN 1-878843-51-6

Edited and published by:
Bev Norwood

Designed by:
Davis Design

Written by:
Melanie Hauser
Helen Ross
Dave Shedloski

Photography by:
PGA TOUR (Chris Condon, Sam
Greenwood, Caryn Levy, Mary Schilpp)
WireImage/Getty Images (David Cannon,
Scott Halleran, Streeter Lecka)
Back cover and page 4 photographs by
Stan Badz, PGA TOUR/WireImage

Color Retouching by:
Luciano Retouching Services, Inc.

Printed in the USA by:
Worzalla Publishing Co.